Roy Willia[m]

Plays: 2

The Gift, Club[.]
Sing Yer Heart Out for the Lads

The Gift: 'Vibrant, sensual and witty.' *Telegraph*

Clubland: 'A slice of life . . . hard and cool.' *Sunday Times*

Sing Yer Heart Out for the Lads: 'An alarming, important bulletin about London today.' *Evening Standard*

Roy Williams worked as an actor before turning to writing full-time in 1990. He graduated from Rose Bruford in 1995 with a first class BA Hons degree in Writing and participated in the 1997 Carlton Television screenwriters' course. *The No Boys Cricket Club* (Theatre Royal, Stratford East, 1996) won him nominations for the TAPS Writer of the Year Award 1996 and for New Writer of the Year 1996 by the Writers' Guild of Great Britain. He was the first recipient of the Alfred Fagon Award 1997 for *Starstruck* (Tricycle Theatre, London, 1998), which also won the 31st John Whiting Award and the EMMA Award 1999. *Lift Off* (Royal Court Theatre Upstairs, 1999) was the joint winner of the George Devine Award 2000. His other plays include: *Night and Day* (Theatre Venture, 1996); *Josie's Boys* (Red Ladder Theatre Co., 1996); *Souls* (Theatre Centre, 1999); *Local Boy* (Hampstead Theatre, 2000); *The Gift* (Birmingham Rep/Tricycle Theatre, 2000); *Clubland* (Royal Court, 2001), winner of the *Evening Standard* Charles Wintour Award for Most Promising Playwright; *Fallout* (2003); and *Sing Yer Heart Out for the Lads* National Theatre, 2002–2004). His screenplays include *Offside* and *Babyfather*  and his radio plays include *Tell Tale* and *Homeboys*, which was broadcast as part of the Radio First Bite Young Writers' Festival. He also wrote *Babyfather* for BBC TV.

by the same author

Roy Williams Plays: 1
(The No Boys Cricket Club, Starstruck, Lift Off)

Fall Out

ROY WILLIAMS

Plays: 2

The Gift

Clubland

Sing Yer Heart Out for the Lads

with a foreword by the author

Methuen Drama

Published by Methuen 2004

1 3 5 7 9 10 8 6 4 2

First published in 2004 by
Methuen Publishing Limited
215 Vauxhall Bridge Road,
London, SW1V 1EJ

Methuen Publishing Limited Reg. No. 3543167

A CIP catalogue record for this book is available from the British Library

ISBN 0 413 77426 0

Typeset by SX Composing DTP, Rayleigh, Essex
Printed and bound in Great Britain
by Cox & Wyman Ltd, Reading, Berkshire

Caution

Contents

Chronology   vii

Foreword   ix

THE GIFT   1

CLUBLAND   59

SING YER HEART OUT FOR THE LADS   129

Roy Williams:
A Chronology

1996   *Night and Day* (Theatre Venture tour)
       The No Boys Cricket Club (Theatre Royal, Stratford
       East). Nominated for the TAPS Writer of the Year
       award 1996 and Writers' Guild Best New Writer
       award 1996.
       Josie's Boys (Red Ladder Theatre Co.)
       Homeboys. Broadcast as part of the BBC Radio 4
       First Bite Young Writers' Festival

1998   *Starstruck* (Tricycle Theatre, London). Received the
       first Alfred Fagon Award, the 31st John Whiting
       Award and the EMMA Award 1999.

1999   *Lift Off* (Royal Court at the Ambassadors). Joint
       winner of the George Devine Award 2000.

2000   *Souls* (Theatre Centre tour)
       Local Boy (Hampstead Theatre)
       The Gift (Birmingham Repertory Theatre,
       transferred to Tricycle Theatre)

2001   *Clubland* (Royal Court Theatre Upstairs). Won the
       Evening Standard Charles Wintour Award for Most
       Promising Playwright.

2002   *Sing Yer Heart Out for the Lads* (National Theatre,
       Lyttelton Loft)
       Writer in Residence, Royal Court Theatre
       Offside (BBC Television). Winner of the BAFTA
       award for best schools drama.
       Babyfather (BBC Television)
       Tell Tale (BBC Radio 4)

2003   *Fallout* (Royal Court Theatre, Downstairs). Received
       the South Bank Show Arts Council Decibel Award.

2004   Revival of *Sing Yer Heart Out for the Lads* at the
       Cottesloe space, National Theatre.

Foreword

To those that know me very well, this will not come as a surprise: I love football! It's my second love – after theatre, of course. My team is Queens Park Rangers. Eight years ago, they were one of the best London teams in the Premiership (don't laugh!). At the time of writing, they're in Division Two, but I'm confident enough that my lads will be back in the top flight before too long. To me, a good game of footie is like seeing a good piece of theatre. They can both be exciting, tense, exhilarating, with a kick-arse, nail-biting finale. However, not all football matches are memorable, much like a lot of plays.

In 2000, my play *The Gift*, the first play in this collection, was running at the Birmingham Rep. The last performance clashed with England playing Germany in the European Championships. The match was televised live. So which did I choose, the play or the match? I chose the match, and I didn't feel guilty about it – I already knew that the play was transferring to London the following month. I found a nice pub in Birmingham city centre with a suitably big telly, settled down with my beer, and readied myself for the match. I was hoping for no trouble, either on or off the field. Sadly, England football fans were making the papers for all the wrong reasons again, doing their country proud by rioting in the streets. The pub seemed nice, relaxed and friendly, but that all changed five minutes before kick-off, when a bunch of young lads came storming in. They were all fans, of course, half drunk and very loud. Most of them were wearing England sweaters and colours, so it was not hard to work out who they were rooting for. They were chanting, singing, screaming every racist word they could think of for a German whenever a German player got the ball.

The match finished with England winning 1–0, an Alan Shearer goal. I was dead happy, but those fans did spoil it for me a little; what is it about a football match that brings out the worst in the English? However, I couldn't help but think that a bunch of fans watching a match in a pub, a closed space, would make a strong image on stage. I mixed those thoughts with the ideas I already had. I very much wanted to write a bigger play, not just simply about race, but about British Nationalism: what does it mean to be British in the twenty-first century, who's more British now, the blacks or the whites? I had been wanting to write about these themes ever since I watched (for the hundredth time) Spike Lee's brilliant movie *Do the Right Thing*, the most honest piece of drama I have ever seen about race. Many pieces of drama (stage or screen) that address racial issues lose their bottle and drown themselves with wishy-washy liberal platitudes. To me, Spike's movie said 'fuck' to all that. It just told it as it was. No apologies.

That is what I wanted for my play. As soon as I got back home, I put pen to paper. Within minutes, *Sing Yer Heart Out for the Lads* was born. It was not an easy play to write. One of the main characters is called Alan. He is a member of a fascist political party, not unlike our British National Party. It was important to me not to make him a devil. I wanted him to be charming, cool, and able to completely justify what he says. The night after *Sing Yer Heart Out* opened, local elections were taking place all over the country. The British National Party won several seats. People were actually going out to vote for them. What was that about? What was it the BNP said that made them do that? It had to be something. It had to come from somewhere. As much as Alan's views disgust me, he does say one thing in the play that I totally agree with:

> . . . if you want to stop people from being like me, then you are going to have to start listening to people like me . . .

That pretty much sums up how I feel racial issues should be addressed. Listen, then confront. No apologies.

Clubland is my most personal play out of the three. I based it heavily on my experiences going out with my mates clubbing in my twenties. I was in a club in South London with them once. I had gone to the gents to relieve myself. Inside there was a bunch of white lads acting a little suspiciously. I didn't ask what they were doing, and I didn't care; I just wanted a piss. Imagine my surprise when one of the guys, shouts to the others, 'Oops, stand back, boys, he's about to embarrass us.' I knew exactly what he meant. I laughed it off, and thought nothing of it as I stepped to the nearest urinal. Imagine my even bigger surprise when the same loud mouth stands next to me, with his face staring right down at my penis, then shouts, 'Ain't that big. I thought you all had big ones.' I didn't say a word; I zipped up, washed my hands, then left. It made me laugh then, but sad that some people still believed in that bullshit. It was sadder when I would see other black guys on the dancefloor, playing up to the myth as they tried to get off with as many white women as possible. Now, I have to hold my hands up here. I was not exactly the perfect gentleman myself back then. Like my mates, I had a condom in my wallet in case I got lucky. Like some of those black guys, I wanted to play the role of a virile well-endowed black man. However, I found myself believing another myth: all white girls are easy and want to be shagged by black men.

It was important to me that I wrote a play that questioned that lifestyle. I really wanted to get into the mind of this particular group of black men. Their insecurities, frustrations; why do they think the only good tool they have is between their legs? *Like Sing Yer Heart Out, Clubland* asks a lot of questions on the issues of cultural identity. Instead of asking what does it mean to be British in today's Britain, *Clubland* was asking what does it mean to be black, who's the blackest – the one who sleeps with over a hundred women, or the one who does not at all? Where do all these stereotypes come from? I know where they come from – society, media, blah blah blah; I was more interested in asking questions like, why does this particular group of black guys play up to this role? Why white women? Is this their way of being accepted by the dominant white culture? These were uncomfortable questions I found hard to ignore. A play had to be written. Cue: *Clubland*.

The Gift is my final play in my trilogy of pieces set in Jamaica. It began with *The No Boys Cricket Club*, followed by *Starstruck*, which can be read in *Plays: 1*. The idea came from chatting with my eldest brother Mark one time. He reminded me that he first came over to England when he was fourteen, in 1966. Like most West Indians, our mum and dad came to this country first. The plan was they would find work and a place to live, and then once they'd settled, send for the kids who would be staying with relatives back home. What I found extraordinary was that sometimes it could be years before these children would see their parents again. That was the case for my brother Mark, who not only had to get used to living in a different country, but also to living with parents who he did not know, who themselves were still getting used to living here. That was a lot for a fourteen-year-old boy to be dealing with. A little while later, my sister Karen joined them and she had to go through the same thing. I found there were many other West Indian children with similar experiences as my brother and sister. I found that much was written about the 'wind rush' generation, and then after that it would be all about their children who were born here, like myself. But little was said about Mark, Karen and the others. To me, they were the 'lost generation' and from then on I was compelled to write a play that told their story.

I wanted to see what kind of parents those kids would become. As with *Starstruck* and *No Boys*, I wanted to continue with my study of the long-term disruption of emigration, the pain of separation when the central character Heather leaves Jamaica while her sister Bernice does not; her struggles of living here and how it affects her children; Bernice's feelings of inferiority when she is left behind; and the ignominy of Heather who believes she is crawling back home with little to show for her years away. In the play, Heather describes her shock when she arrived in England from Jamaica as a teenager to meet a father she no longer recognised. Heather climbs to the top of her tree to become a doctor and tries to bully her children into doing the same. The play begins with Heather returning home to bury her son Andrew, who was killed in a street fight, while her drop-out daughter Janet and jealous sister Bernice, who believes she can talk to the dead, both carp from the side. Heather has driven her kids to do well. She does not want them to have a cap in their hands, waiting for the dominant white culture to save them. She is right, but also wrong. She is not letting them become who they want to be. The sub-plot of Andrew's spirit haunting them comes from my side interest in the supernatural. Most cultures have stories of ghosts and spirits; the Caribbean is no different.

As ever, much love to my family and all the friends and colleagues who have helped me with my career (see *Plays: 1* for a full checklist). A big kiss to all the cast and crew who worked on these three plays. The biggest thanks have to go to three geniuses: Annie Castledine for directing a beautiful production of *The Gift*; Simon Usher for his brilliant work on *Sing Yer Heart Out for the Lads*; and, of course, my 'little big sister' Indhu Rubasingham for doing such a cracking job on *Clubland*. A new play is only as good as the person who directs it. With you guys at the helm, my plays had the best.

Roy Williams
February 2004

The Gift

Characters

Bernice
Heather
Janet
Clarkey

Setting
Clarendon, Jamaica

Note
Bernice and Heather are both fifteen years old in the first scene and in their late forties thereafter.

Scene One

A graveyard, Clarendon, Jamaica. Afternoon. **Bernice**, *fifteen, comes running on. She looks inside a small grave that hasn't been filled yet.*

Bernice (*whispers*) She soon come.

She looks around quickly before deciding where to hide. **Heather**, *also fifteen, comes running on. She looks around suspiciously for* **Bernice**. **Heather** *does not notice* **Bernice** *creeping up behind her.* **Bernice** *grabs* **Heather** *from behind.*

Bernice Slip yu!

Heather Slip yu back!

Bernice Yu can't slip mi back.

Heather Why not?

Bernice Ca I awready slip yu, game finish Header, mi win.

Heather It nuh finish.

Bernice It finish.

Heather Yu go tell mi we play best outta three.

Bernice And dis is de third.

Heather Second, yu so stupid.

Bernice Third. Don't talk like I fool girl.

Heather Well don't act like fool.

Bernice We were playin' slip outside yer house an hour ago, Clarkey was deh remember?

Heather Dat weren't a go.

Bernice Shut yer mout'.

Heather It were not. We were jus' showin' Clarkey how to play de game.

Bernice   An' we did. We played it fer trut', right? Third go, I win.

Heather   Nossir.

Bernice   Fine den. Gwan wid yerself, for de rest a' de day.

Heather   Bernice, is why yu love to moan?

Bernice   Header, is why yu love to cheat?

Heather   I don't cheat, it not my fault yu can't count.

Bernice   I can count!

Heather   Yu don' go school, everybody know dat. Yu can' even read.

Bernice   I can read!

Heather   Yeah like sum fool, like Connie Williams, yu come jus' like she, fall on yer head when she a baby.

Bernice   An' yu tink yu so clever?

Heather   Mi know.

Bernice   Yer fart.

Heather   I get two As for history an' math, Bernice, two! Is how many yu ever get?

Bernice   When yu say yer leavin'?

Heather   Four o'clock.

Bernice   Yu wan' live till den?

Heather   Touch mi I tell mi mudda.

Bernice   Yu tell yer mudda, I go put spell on yu, mek all hair fall out next mornin'.

Heather   Yer fart!

Bernice   Every bit a' it.

Heather   Leave mi alone, right?

Bernice (*laughs*)   Fool. Yu believe mi.

Heather   I never say I believe yu.

Bernice   Yer face do.

Heather   Mi can't wait to get away from yu.

Bernice   I can't wait fer yu to get away from mi.

Heather   Yu mean yu won't miss me.

Bernice   Nope.

Heather   Yu lie.

Bernice   So why yu ask mi?

Heather   Why yu so nasty to mi?

Bernice   Yu nasty to mi.

Heather   Yu will miss mi, won't yu Bernice? I is never go ferget yu Bernice.

Bernice   Yu too lie.

Heather   Mi nuh lie.

Bernice   As soon as yu arrive in England, yu is gonna ferget all about mi. Jus' like everybody else. Everyone ferget 'bout Bernice.

Heather   I won't.

Bernice   Lie!

Heather   I hate yu, yu nuh!

Bernice   Hate yu too.

Heather *bursts into tears.*

Bernice   Oh come on, don't even tink 'bout dat Header Stuart. Jus' no budda. Wat, yu get A in acting as well? Stop it. Yu nuh hear wat mi say, stop it. Yu love to tek joke too far Header! Awright, awright, I go miss yu too, but only a lickle, right?

Heather   Lickle?

Bernice   Awright a lot. Child I go miss yu a lot. Now stop yer cryin'.

Heather (*with great ease*)   Awright den! (*Laughs.*)

Bernice   Yu lickle rass yu!

Heather (*chants*)   Yu say yu love mi, yu say yu love mi . . .

Bernice   Nasty lickle bitch.

Heather   Yu wan' sum advice Bernice, yu wan' be smart like mi, go back to school, mi mudda go school, an' look, two a' we go on a plane, fly to England. Or yu want stay on dis island, and grow stupid?

Bernice   Move from mi.

Heather   Yu wan' cry Bernice.

Bernice   Yu and yer mudda think yu so better than we.

Heather   Because we are.

Bernice   Carry on, gwan like she.

Heather   I will.

Bernice   Let's si how high and mighty she is living in Englan'.

Heather   We go live in a big house, we go have servants. Daddy say in him last letter.

Bernice   Him nuh say dat.

Heather   How yu know?

Bernice   Yu tell mi las' time yu hear from him, him get job working in factory, ware dem mek tele.

Heather   Yes.

Bernice   But now him have enough to have servants?

Heather   Yes.

Bernice   So tell mi summin, how come my mudda's cousin Frankie, who also go England, tell mi mudda dat he bump into yer daddy, deh work in de same place, and cousin Frankie him nuh have no servants.

Heather   Shut yer mout'.

Bernice   Yu tell so much lie. One day yer nose grow so big, it go drop off. I'm glad we stayin' here.

Heather   I go live in Putney.

Bernice   Putney?

Heather   It's in London.

Bernice   Sound like summin yu put between two slices a' bread.

Bernice *takes out a large cigar and lights it.*

Heather   Is ware de hell yu get dat?

Bernice   Mi find it.

Heather   Inside Grandaddy's jacket is ware yu find it. Him favourite cigars dat, yu nuh.

Heather   Give it back.

Bernice   Move.

Heather   It nuh belong to yu.

Bernice   Yu want fight yer cousin Header?

Heather   Keep de stupid cigar, Granddaddy away smell bad anyhow. Mama away mek him smoke outside de house.

Bernice *blows smoke in her face.*

Heather   Move! Let mi have a smoke? (*Takes the cigar.*) I miss him yu nuh Bernice.

Bernice   Who?

Heather   Dadda.

Bernice How can yu miss 'im, yu only lickle when 'im go, yu can't remember 'im.

Heather Don't mean I can't miss 'im, ware it say I can't miss 'im? And I do remember 'im, wid his big smile an 'im gold tooth. First ting I do when mi get to Englan', I go give him a big hug yu si. I go hold him, never let go.

Bernice My turn! (*Snatches the cigar.*)

Heather (*protests*) Hey!

Bernice Watch mi now. (*Blows smoke rings.*)

Heather It's cold. Yu nuh feel cold?

Bernice We in a grave field.

Heather Yeah, but dat no reason to feel cold though. Wat was dat?

Bernice Wat was wat?

Heather Dat gust a' wind. Yu nuh feel it?

Bernice Must be de spirits.

Heather Duppies?

Bernice Deh all around us.

Heather Dem dead.

Bernice Dem tortured spirits Header.

Heather Yu too lie.

Bernice Caught between worlds.

Heather Which worlds?

Bernice Dis world and de oder life, yu so stupid.

Heather Yu stupid!

Bernice Yu afraid?

Heather No.

Bernice   Yu want talk to dem?

Heather   Shut yer mout' Bernice.

Bernice   I thought yu say yu not afraid.

Heather   I'm not.

Bernice   Come on den.

Heather   Yu can't talk to ghosts!

Bernice   Den yu got nuttin to be afraid of.

Heather   Awright. Gwan den. If yu can.

Bernice   So who yu want to speak to, Grandma? Uncle Sammy? Yer old dog Sparkey?

Heather   How de hell can I speak to a dog?

Bernice   Uncle Sammy den.

Heather   How yu go do this?

Bernice   Watch.

Bernice *kneels beside Sammy's grave. She places her hand on the grave and closes her eyes. She slowly begins to chant.*

Heather (*laughs*)   Come on Bernice, enough is enough. Bernice, Bernice! I don't believe yu. Stop it, I not scared, right? Stop it!

Bernice (*in another voice*)   Header Stuart!

Heather *shrieks.*

Bernice   Yu bin a good girl, Header?

Heather   Stop it Bernice. Yu love to tek joke too far.

Bernice   Bernice? Who dat?

Heather   Uncle Sammy?

Bernice   Yu bin a good girl fer yer mudda, Header?

Heather   Yes, Uncle Sammy.

Bernice   Wat yu doin' wid yerself?

Heather   I going to England, Uncle Sammy. To live. I go si mi daddy.

Bernice   Yer daddy? Him a good man, Header. Mind yu tek care a' him.

Heather   Yes, Uncle Sammy.

Bernice   Yu sure yu bin a good girl, Header?

Heather   Yes.

Bernice   So wa 'appen to mi dog Sparkey?

Heather   Him get sick, Uncle Sammy.

Bernice   Don't lie to mi girl.

Heather   She run into de road, Uncle Sammy, get hit by car. I try to hold on, but she too quick.

Bernice   Yu kill my dog?

Heather   No, Uncle Sammy.

Bernice   When I ask yu to tek care a' her.

Heather   Mi sorry.

Bernice   It awright Heather. It not yer fault yu kill mi dog. Come outta deh Sparkey.

Heather   Bernice can yu hear mi girl?

Bernice   Sparkey! Him comin'. Come to mi Sparkey.

Noise comes from the open grave.

Heather   I wan' go home.

Clarkey *jumps out of the grave.* **Heather** *screams.* **Clarkey** *chases her.* **Heather** *runs in fear but eventually stops when she recognises the person chasing her.*

Heather   Clarkey!

Clarkey   Yu turn whiter dan white Header! (*Barks like a dog, runs off.*)

Heather   Yu nasty evil lickle wretch Clarkey, I hate yu!

Heather *turns to see* **Bernice** *laughing her head off.*

Heather   Yu trick mi.

Bernice   Yu trick yerself. Why yu so stupid, Header?

Heather   I'm not stupid. I'm not!

Bernice   Yu go cry now? It was only a joke. It were Clarkey's idea.

Heather   Clarkey a dog, 'im do wat yu tell 'im.

Bernice   Don't go yet. I only wanted to give yu summin to remember us by. I go miss yu, Header.

Heather   Yu love to lie.

Bernice   I go miss yu. More dan yu realise. We is family Header.

Heather   Mi know!

Bernice   We is sisters.

Heather   Shut up.

Bernice   Yer daddy is my daddy.

Heather   I'll punch yu hard, yu nuh.

Bernice   Both our muddas were fightin' las' night, I hear dem. I hear de trut'.

Heather   Why yu love to lie?

Bernice   Yu shoulda hear my mudda scream, it wake de dead. Yer daddy sleep wid him dead brudda's wife!

Heather   No!

Bernice   It trut'.

Heather   No!

Sound of a dog growling.

Bernice   Wat were dat?

Heather   Bernice!

Bernice   It not mi.

Heather   Sparkey?

Dog barks.

Heather\Bernice   Jesus!

The girls run for their lives.

Scene Two

Present day. The same graveyard.

Heather *is alone. She is standing over a new grave. She kneels down over the flat headstone. She sweeps the dust off the headstone with her hands, then replaces the flowers with fresh ones.*

Heather   There you are, son.

Janet *(enters)*   Tell yer Mum yu don't half walk fast. Didn't yu hear me calling yer? Mum?

Heather *can hear her daughter but does not reply.* **Janet** *just stands for a moment, watching her mother, not saying anything. She finally goes over when she can hear her mother crying.*

Janet   Yu want a tissue?

Heather   No. You keep them, you need them.

Janet   I aint sneezed since we got here.

Heather   Don't tempt fate, Janet.

Janet   Mus' be the clean air.

Heather   You call this clean? Did you think the house was clean when we got there? Or was that my imagination?

Janet   No Mum.

Heather   I'm going to kill Bernice when I see her. How hard is it to meet us at the airport, how hard is that?

Janet   She sent Clarkey.

Heather   Clarkey sent himself. He's bin covering for her since school.

Janet   He's really sweet aint he?

Heather   He's not a dog, Janet.

Janet *sneezes.*

Heather   See, that is you tempting fate.

Janet   Bloody hell.

Heather   Come on.

Janet   Ware's my tissue? (*Searches for tissue and continues to sneeze.*)

Heather (*can't bear to look*)   Hurry up.

Janet   It's not my fault.

Heather   I can't bear to look at you when you are like this.

Janet   So don't look.

Heather   Why do you always sneeze?

Janet   I got allergies.

Heather   And every five minutes you have a cold. I bet you don't eat any vegetables at all, do you?

Janet   Yeah.

Heather   You are puttin' on weight.

Janet (*feeling embarrassed*)   Mum!

Heather   Go on a diet.

Janet   Diets don't work.

Heather   You don't work. You've got no discipline. I can draw up a balanced diet for you if you want.

Janet   No thanks. (*Stops sneezing. Blows her nose. Looks down at it afterwards.*)

Heather (*disgusted*)   Don't look at it! You're not pregnant again are you?

Janet   Wat yu mean again? Yu carry on like I'm dropping them every five minutes. No I'm not.

Heather   Then you are putting on weight.

Janet   Awright then I am.

Heather   You carry on like this my dear, you'll end up like those big, fat, awful women that never leave their houses.

Janet   Oh stop it.

Heather   They just sit down all day watching tele and stuffing their faces all day, the slobs.

Janet   Fine.

Heather   Look at your grandmother.

Janet   Oh leave her alone. Gran aint no slob.

Heather   I know, but see how slow she walks now. Why do you think she never came with us? You have a good look at her when you see her next, Janet. That is what happens when you reach the end . . .

Janet   Yu are so out of order.

Heather   . . . when you let yourself go. Diet! It won't kill you to try.

Janet   I'll try. (*Looks around.*) So this is it? Our family. Am I gonna end up here as well?

Heather   Ignore her, son.

Janet   Sorry broth, I'm jus' makin' bad jokes again. Peace. (*Spots a headstone.*) Sparkey? Who's that?

Heather   Come away from there, Janet.

Janet   Cousin, uncle?

Heather   Come away from there.

Janet   Wat? Yer as white as a sheet, man.

Heather   Don't be so stupid.

Janet   Look in a mirror if yu don't believe me.

Heather   Sparkey was my dog.

Janet   Yu had a dog?

Heather   Obviously.

Janet   Yu hate dogs.

Heather   I know.

Janet   Remember when I was eight, yu wouldn't let me have one.

Heather   Yes.

Janet   Wat 'appened to it?

Heather   It got hit by a car.

Janet   Sorry. Funeral went well.

Heather   It wasn't enough. The pastor didn't know him. What did he know about Andrew and his life?

Janet   Yu wanted him buried here.

Heather   I didn't want him buried there.

Janet   Yu can't blame a whole country for wat happened.

Heather   How english of yu.

Janet   We're not the only ones who missed him. All his mates wanted to say goodbye.

Heather   They had the memorial service to do that.

Janet   That was last year.

Heather   This was our service. The family.

Janet   Yeah, and wat about Dad?

Heather   What about him? If he cared, he'd be here.

Janet   He doesn't even know, Mum.

Heather   What do you want me to do, traipse through the whole of America to find him?

Janet   No.

Heather   He doesn't want to be found.

Janet   I'm jus' . . .

Heather   . . . You don't know that by now?

Janet   Awright forget it!

Heather (*clocks her daughter's face*)   Don't do that.

Janet   Don't do wat?

Heather   That look.

Janet   Wat look?

Heather   The same look your father used to pull.

Janet   I'm not Dad, awright?

Heather   So lose the look.

Janet   Jesus!

Heather   Janet why have you come here?

Janet   He was my brother, Mum.

Heather   No, why have you followed me here?

Janet (*sarcastic*)   I fancied a walk. To see if yer awright.

Heather   Well I am, so you can go back to the house and call your boyfriend now.

Janet   Ryan. Can't yu say his name just once?

Heather   Maybe if you had stayed in school . . .

Janet (*knows what is coming*)   . . . No!

Heather   . . . instead of skiving off with your worthless friends, trying to run a restaurant with your aimless boyfriend . . . getting yourself pregnant.

Janet   Oh yu had to bloody go there. (*Smug.*) Don't do that.

Heather   Don't do what?

Janet   That look.

Heather (*getting defensive*)   What look?

Janet   The disappointed look.

Heather (*getting wound up*)   Child!

Janet   Yu don't believe me, fine, I don't care.

Heather *raises her hands. She has had enough of this.*

Heather   I'll come back later, son.

Janet (*pleads with her*)   Oh Mum!

Heather *leaves.*

Janet (*to the grave*)   Summin I said? Wat about yu then, yu got summin to say? Don't talk to Mum like that, yer embarrassed to be my brother? Like I don't know? Yu aint exactly wat I had in mind for a big brother yu know? (*Laughs.*) 'Yu ever see Andrew do that?' She aint seen half the things yu've done, ennit broth? I know wat yer tryin' to do. Well yu can piss off. Yu weren't nice to me either, I'm supposed to drain my tears over yu, little mummy's boy? Move! All I have to do is tell her right, jus' open my mouth, let her know wat her precious little boy was really like, yu think I won't . . .

A gust of wind comes sweeping through.

Janet (*feels something*) Broth?

Scene Three

Outside **Bernice**'s.

Clarkey *is with* **Bernice**.

Clarkey   Drink it.

Bernice   No man.

Clarkey   Drink it!

Bernice   Move yerself!

Clarkey   Yu wan' stay drunk all day?

Bernice   Clarkey, I'd rather be drunk dan drink wat yu call tea!

Clarkey   Yu turn up yer nose at mi mudda's home-made tea?

Bernice   Clarkey, no offence right, but it nasty!

Clarkey   Fine den!

Bernice   Oh Clarkey man!

Clarkey   Yu wan' feel like shit, gwan!

Bernice   Relax man, a joke mi a mek. Smile nuh man!

Clarkey   Mi nuh feel like it.

Bernice   Wat mi do?

Clarkey   Ware de hell yu bin, Bernice?

Bernice   Lord Jesus, I go down Kingston to si Judy.

Clarkey   Yu nuh even tell mi.

Bernice   Oh we marry now?

Clarkey   Yu jus' gwan. It's mi the one who have to pick up yer sister Bernice, mi never feel so shame in all mi life.

Bernice   Oh shush.

Clarkey   Shameful!

Bernice   Shush! Deh settle in?

Clarkey   No tanks to yu.

Bernice   Yes mi hear yu now.

Clarkey   Jus' about.

Bernice   How is she?

Clarkey   She seem awright. I tell yu if it were mi, man, I dunno if I coulda speak. Yu shoulda bin here to greet her, Bernice.

Bernice   Awright nuh man! Is why yu love to chat so?

Clarkey   So wat yu do dat so important in Kingston?

Bernice   Yu nosey eeh!

Clarkey   Yu go tell mi?

Bernice   I go si Judy like mi say.

Clarkey   And?

Bernice   And wat?

Clarkey   No tell mi no fish stories right.

Bernice   Oooh, Clarkey big man now!

Clarkey   Woman!

Bernice   Awright! But yu go get mad.

Clarkey   Jus' tell mi.

Bernice   Judy have a friend, right? She live downtown an' las' week her daddy dead.

Clarkey   Huh huh?

Bernice   But him leave behind a whole heap of bills, soon deh get thrown outta de house.

Clarkey   Wat dis have to do wid yu?

Bernice   Wait nuh! But before de daddy dead right, he leave sum big insurance policy, but dem can't find it, deh search all over de house, cursing deh daddy name while deh doin' it, ca' when he was alive, he was shrewd, too shrewd fer him own good. Him love him secret hidin' places to put away him tings, no one knows ware he leave de policy.

Clarkey   So why he never tell dem ware de policy is?

Bernice   Ca' him never know he go get lick in de head by sum mule las' month and die next day. Fool! Him must tink him go die by gettin' old and sick, dat way him got time to tell him family an' wat deh have to do.

Clarkey   Is ware yu come into dis?

Bernice   Judy tell dem about mi.

Clarkey   And?

Bernice   And deh ask if I coulda contact de fudda, find out ware him hide de policy.

Clarkey   I knew it!

Bernice   Eighty dollars deh give mi Clarkey.

Clarkey   Yu never learn.

Bernice   Oh shut up.

Clarkey   So yu talk to him?

Bernice   Yeah man, mi hear 'im.

Clarkey *shakes his head.*

Bernice Mi hear 'im, man!

Clarkey So ware 'im hide de policy?

Bernice 'Im nuh tell mi, and before yu gimme any of yer stupid look right, 'im say he not go tell ca' 'im accuse 'im 'ole family a' bin gravedigger, deh nuh care 'bout him when 'im alive, so why 'im should care now 'im dead?

Clarkey I jus' hope yu give dem back deh money.

Bernice Yu such a boy scout, yu nuh.

Clarkey I'd rather be dat dan sum wort'less tief.

Bernice I don't tief, I provide a service. Bernice Stuart, spiritualist advisor.

Clarkey I bet deh catch yu out ennit? Deh find out and chase yu outta Kingston?

Bernice No.

Clarkey Deh nuh hurt yu, right?

Bernice Nuttin 'appened. Mi fine.

Clarkey Downtown a rough place, Bernice.

Bernice I got de gift, Clarkey.

Clarkey *shakes his head.*

Bernice Oh yu mek mi so mad.

Clarkey Mi mek yu drunk too? Yu tink yu go find wat yu wan' at de bottom of de bottle?

Bernice Yu not mi mudda.

Clarkey Nor are yu.

Bernice Awright! Yu jus' shut yer mout'. Yu cross the line now.

Clarkey An' yu too old to farm de fool.

Bernice Oh cha rass man.

Clarkey   It nuh right.

Bernice   Yu go tell mi wat is?

Clarkey   Yu know.

Bernice   Marry yu. Be a mudda to yer wort'less son, lookin' after yer sick mudda. Clarkey mi dunno if I ready fer all dat.

Clarkey   Woman yu is forty-seven now, forty-seven. If yu don't know, is when?

Bernice   Wat yu si in mi Clarkey? Why yu want fer marry mi? Yu better off wid Junie Riley, she aways like yu.

Clarkey   Junie Riley only have one eye, an' she can't si nuh better wid dat one.

Bernice   Remember when she walk right in Miss Devereaux's shop? (*Laughs.*) Straight through de window she go, like sum fool.

Clarkey   Woman can't even look after she self let alone my mudda.

Bernice   Si, deh yu go, yu want nursemaid.

Clarkey   If yu coulda let mi finish, yu never let mi finish.

Bernice   Sorry.

Clarkey   It's not she mi love.

Bernice   Yu is a good man Clarkey . . .

Clarkey   . . . Don't say dat.

Bernice   And yu gwan 'bout not lettin' yu finish.

Clarkey   Sorry.

Bernice   I need more time, man.

Clarkey   How much more time yu need?

Enter **Janet** *with bags of shopping.*

Clarkey (*points to Bernice*)   Well look who mi find.

Janet   Hello Auntie.

Bernice   Lickle Janet is dat yu? Girl yu get round, yu nuh.

Janet   Yu awright?

Bernice   Mi fine darling, fine! Look at yu now. Is why yu stand so far? Mi nuh bite, much. Come. (*Gives her a hug.*) Lickle Janet! Awright den, so ware mi beautiful lickle great niece, Tamia right? Ware she den?

Janet   Back home wid her dad.

Bernice   Oh yu shoulda bring her, child. Mi can't wait to see her. It so good to have yu all here. Sorry mi not here to greet yu, and de state of de house, an' there were no food, yer auntie had tings to do, yu nuh. She a busy woman, yu know how it is.

Janet   Don't worry about it.

Clarkey   Don't go feelin' sorry fer her, Janet. Mek her feel bad, it wat she deserve.

Bernice   Yes tank yu, Clarkey.

Clarkey   Who want sum tea?

Bernice   Say no.

Clarkey   Mi hear dat. (*Goes inside.*)

Bernice   Janet look at yu! How long it bin?

Janet   I dunno, ages. I was still at school.

Bernice   Look 'pon yu! Yu is a woman now. Mudda. Yu still have man? Wat him name?

Janet   Ryan.

Bernice   Oooh Ryan! 'Im fit? (*Roars.*) It's awright, long as yu hang on to him tail dough, before sum oder gal come drag 'im away, like mi. Smile Janet, mi mek joke.

Janet   I know.

Bernice (*acting really offended*)   Wat yu mean yu know? Yu don't tink I can get man? Listen right, yer auntie have more dan she fair share of fit young man, and I mean fit! Right? (*Bursts out laughing.*) Child listen right, if yu want spend time wid mi, yu have to loosen up, yu hear? Nuh come like yer mudda, mi beg yu.

Janet *does not quite get* **Bernice***'s sense of humour.* **Bernice** *laughs again.*

Bernice   Lord, yu english fer trut'. (*Turns serious.*) Look, listen right, I so sorry about Andy.

Janet   Thanks Auntie.

Bernice   He was a lovely bwai Janet. Brock my heart when I hear de news, brock my heart.

Janet   Yeah.

Heather *enters.*

Bernice   MADAME!

Heather   Shown yourself at last then have you?

Bernice   How yu doin' sister?

Heather   I'm doing fine, Bernice.

Bernice   Yu have no big sisterly hug fer mi?

Heather   Don't be ridiculous.

Bernice   Come let mi hold yu.

Heather   You stay where you are.

Bernice   Come nuh! (*Grabs her, lifts her up.*)

Heather (*protests*)   Bernice!

Bernice   Gal yu get heavy!

Heather   So put me down.

Bernice *obeys.*

Heather   Now let me go.

Bernice   No.

Heather   What do you mean no?

Bernice   Yu nuh say de magic word.

Heather   Will you *please* let me go.

Bernice (*thinks about it for a second*)   No.

Heather   I said the magic word.

Bernice   Mi happy to si yu!

Heather (*pleads*)   Bernice!

Bernice (*releases her*)   Oh yes, mi ferget yu turn english now.

Heather   Where the hell have you been?

Bernice   I jus' love de way yu talk now, yu si.

Heather (*putting on the accent*)   Is ware yu bin?

Bernice   Around.

Heather   Where?

Bernice   Jus' around.

Janet (*feeling awkward*)   Right then, I'll leave yu two to it, yeah?

Heather   Where are you going?

Janet   Jus' inside, gonna help Clarkey. (*Exits.*)

Bernice   Alone at last, hey?

Heather   Stop it.

Bernice   Come on Header, one more hug?

Heather   Why won't you answer my question?

Bernice   Ca' mi nuh like de question.

Heather   You should have been here.

Bernice   Yu know mi awready Header, can't keep still fer anyting.

Heather   I also know you can't hold a broom in your hand. I can't believe the state you left the house in.

Bernice   It's my house.

Heather   Daddy left it to me, Bernice.

Bernice   And yu love to throw dat in mi face.

Heather   So I don't have a right to speak? I'm supposed to walk around all that mess, and pretend it's not there? Is that right, is that what you are saying? Are you listening to me? (*Sees* **Bernice** *looking at her watch.*) What are you doing?

Bernice   Two minute. We nuh si each oder fer years an' years and it tek two minute fer us to fight.

Heather   Fine, make your jokes.

Bernice   Gimme a chance to say sorry?

Heather   Go on then.

Bernice   I sorry I miss de funeral.

Heather   Did you find something better to do?

Bernice   Fine, I deserve dat.

Heather   That doesn't even come close.

Bernice   Well if yu feel like dat why don't yu jus' go home? Yu done wat yu wan', yu buried yer son, go home.

Heather   You should have been here, that's all I'm saying to you.

Bernice   Why? Yu carry on like yu wan' fer mi to tek care a yu?

Heather   I do not need anyone taking care of me!

Bernice   So wat yu chat 'bout?

Heather   Nothing.

Bernice (*trying to lighten the situation*)   Slip yu?

Heather   Just buy a broom Bernice, one broom.

Bernice   Yu want fer mi to go right now?

Heather   Outside doesn't look much better. Don't you think it's time you painted it again?

Bernice   Nope.

Heather   It's a disgrace.

Bernice   Daddy painted it.

Heather (*surprised*)   Daddy?

Bernice   Is why yu look surprise?

Heather   I didn't know that.

Bernice   Now yu do.

Heather   Back home Mum had to drag Daddy off his couch, beg him to do any work around the house.

Bernice   Well 'im weren't in England when he paint de house.

Heather   I am not here to fight, OK?

Bernice   Den don't talk.

Heather   I'm going inside.

Bernice   Yu carry on like yu dead too.

Heather   I'm tired.

Bernice   Watever yu say, sister.

Scene Four

Graveyard.

Janet *is alone.*

Janet (*laughing*) . . . then she lifted her up, right in the air –
yu shoulda seen it man, Mum's face. Strong man. 'Member
when she told us once, she could pick up a whole horse by
herself? And yu believed her, yer soft git. And yu were
afraid of her, cos she loved tellin' ghost stories, hidin' under
my covers whenever we heard the footsteps. 'Auntie Bernice
is comin' to get me!' That was yu. Scared little Andy, I
remember that, yu fool. Yu know summin, it's weird, right,
but I feel like . . . Andy, yu watchin' me? Andy? Shut the
fuck up Janet. Hear wat, Mum knows 'bout the caff so yu
know wass gonna 'appen now? She gonna go on and on
about it, yu know how she stay, me and Ryan should sell up,
prove her right, Janet's fucked up again. Cos compared to
yu, I'm nuttin, ennit broth? I hate, fuckin' hate yu. I hate
yu. I don't miss yu, wid yer snidy little bitchy comments,
who yu tryin' to impress? Then yu actin' all hard, givin' it
large, wat were yu thinkin' man? Wat was goin' thru yer
head? Now yu tryin' to mek me feel bad, wat yu want?

*She starts stamping on the headstone, she kicks the flowers, picks up
some pebbles and dirt and throws them at it.*

Janet (*in a rage*)   Wat . . .

*She feels the wind again. She turns around suddenly. Someone is there
with her, she can feel it. She can hear something.*

Janet (*terrified*) No.

Scene Five

Outside **Bernice**'s *house.*

Heather *is with* **Clarkey**.

Heather (*laughing*)   No!

Clarkey   It trut'.

Heather   Stop it.

Clarkey   No, listen. Yu remember Teddy Jeffries and him brudda, right? They never get on, right? Yu remember? Argue, Jesus, like cat an' dog.

Heather   I remember them.

Clarkey   So when him brudda dead, Teddy carry like he got no care in de world. Tellin' him wife he go do wat him want, drink and gamble whenever him feel. She say 'Nossir,' him say 'Shut yer mout' woman.' So, him wife decide she go teach him a lesson. She go si Bernice, give her fifty dollars to tell Teddy she si a vision of him brudda, telling him he must give up him bad ways, oderwise him go come back as a black fowl and follow him everywhere till him drop down dead. So Teddy wife get deh bwoy Jody to buy de blackest fowl him si, follow him daddy, no get catch, and mek sure de fowl near him daddy. Den, pass de word all over town, that everybody mus' pretend deh can't si de fowl, it's Teddy's mind ca' him drinkin' too much dat mek him and nobody else si de fowl. It go on fer a whole week, Teddy losin' him mind. 'Wa gwan, wa gwan, lord help mi nuh, mi lose mi mind!'

Heather   So wat did he do?

Clarkey   'Im shoot de fowl! 'Im get him daddy old shotgun an' blast de ting into de next life. Right in the middle a' de street. Him scream, 'Yu all si dat?' Dem si it awright, policeman as well, dem haul 'im arse right into jail. When him find out de trut', Teddy go after him wife, go after him bwoy.

Heather   Bernice?

Clarkey   She hide out in mi yard. It tek a whole month fer Teddy to calm down. I tell yu, Header, dat sister a' yours.

Heather   She want tekin' in hand.

Clarkey   Yu talk like I don't know dat.

Heather   Hurry up man, make a honest woman of her.

Clarkey   It she mi waitin' on. Maybe I should mek joke, and say mi want fer marry yu.

Heather   Yer mad if yu want do that. She'll come round Clarkey.

Clarkey   When mi dead?

Heather   She'll see you.

Clarkey   Si wat?

Heather   That you're a good man.

Clarkey (*cringes*)   Why yu women love to say dat?

Heather   But it's true. You arranged everything for me.

Clarkey   Who else go do it?

Heather   And yu still know how to make me laugh. Only yu, man.

Clarkey   Wat, no one mek yu laugh in Englan'?

Heather *shakes her head.*

Clarkey   Yu nuh laugh at all?

Heather   Not for a while.

Clarkey   I still can't believe it.

Heather   You telling me that?

Clarkey   Him only a lickle bwoy when mi las' si him.

Heather   That's how I try to see him sometimes, as a little boy. Riding on his bike when he was what, eleven. Wearing his Arsenal kit. Do you love your son, Clarkey?

Clarkey   Wort'less wretch!

Heather   But you do love him?

Clarkey   Yeah, so?

Heather   When was the last time you told him that?

Clarkey   (*getting embarrassed*)   Header?

Heather   What?

Clarkey   Come on.

Heather   Is that such a hard question?

Clarkey   Mi can't remember.

Heather   You'll be surprised how many parents say the same thing. They know they love their children, they feel it every day, but they don't say it. Where I live right, I see so many parents, yellin' at their kids, to do this an' that, fighting with them, throwing them out, swearing. You wouldn't believe it man, they haven't got a clue. They don't deserve to have children. It never occurs to them for one minute in their stupid minds, that might be the last thing they ever say to them. Because an hour from now they might get knocked down by a bus, get hurt in a car crash, or get stabbed . . .

Clarkey   Header . . .

Heather   And when that happens? They try to remember all the good things they did with their children, the nice things they said, but the only thing that keeps coming back is the last thing they said to them, the last time they saw them. So angry, full of hate, just for a moment, a split bloody second, but it keeps coming back.

Clarkey   So wat yu want dem parents to do? Tell dem pikne every blasted day deh love dem?

Heather   Why not?

Clarkey   Ca' if I tell Neil I love 'im every day right, all him go do is laugh, an' all I go do is knock off 'm head!

Children are good, Header, but deh also renk! Dass it. Yu can't beat yerself up.

Heather   He wanted to join a band, Clarkey, he wanted to quit college in his final year, and go join a stupid band, I had to say something . . .

Clarkey   Yes.

Heather   I couldn't just sit there and nod my head.

Clarkey   No.

Heather   I didn't raise him to be like his father. He was walking through some seedy little street, thass where Nicholls saw him, where that animal kill him.

Clarkey   No, no, don't.

Heather   He took him from me.

Clarkey   Mi know.

Heather   He got away with it.

Clarkey   Yes.

Heather   And they all jus' stood by and let him do it.

Clarkey   He's a bastard, Header, he's a sunafabitch.

Heather   They're all bastards, Clarkey, they're all sons of bitches. Thirty-two years of my life man, thirty-two years, paying into their system. All I wanted back was justice, not lies, just justice. Andrew never started trouble in his whole life.

Clarkey   Course he didn't.

Heather   I raised him better than that.

Clarkey   Course yu do.

Heather   He was a good boy.

Clarkey   Wat yu go do, Header?

Heather I don't know. As soon as I heard the verdict, all I wanted was to get out of there, get my boy out of there. He was too good for that country anyway.

Clarkey Is why yu nuh stay? Dis yer home gal.

Heather Don't let Bernice hear yu say that.

Clarkey Is who yer daddy leave 'im house to? Dis ware yu belong.

Heather I could go back.

Clarkey Go back fer wat?

Heather Get justice for Andrew. I don't want to feel like I let him down.

Clarkey Shut up, yu nuh let nobody down, right? Yu did yer best.

Heather That's what my mum says. 'I did my best fer yu, Header.'

Clarkey Come on.

Heather I don't know wat I'm doing man, I don't know wat to feel.

Clarkey Yu stay which part yu deh. Yu soon see how yu feel, promise yu. Den we go tek all yer problems yu see, roll dem all up in a ball, kick it right up in de sky, let it go, straight past through de cloud dem. Past de sun, pass de moon, outer space! Yu hearin' mi?

Heather *smiles.*

Clarkey Wat?

Heather Bernice is such an idiot.

Clarkey Gwan tell her, mi nuh stop yu.

Heather Tell me another story, Clarkey. Come on man, make me laugh again.

Bernice *enters, singing. She sees* **Heather** *and* **Clarkey**.

Bernice   Well look 'pon dis! My two favourite people in de whole world, chatting. How nicey, eeh? Nice.

Clarkey   Yu drunk again?

Bernice   Sorry mudda.

Clarkey   I mek sum drink.

Bernice   I don' want nona yer mama's blasted tea, right!

Heather   Bernice!

Bernice   Yu nuh taste it, Header, come like summin outta my behind. Yu wan' drink it? Gwan Clarkey, mek sum fer Heather, gwan.

Clarkey   Should be ashamed.

Bernice   Oh leave mi man. Hey Header, Header, who dis? (*Barks like a dog.*)

Heather   Stop it.

Bernice   Ca' yu know who it is.

Clarkey   Enuff Bernice.

Bernice   Two a' yu carry on like yu old people. (*Mimics.*) Sparkey, Sparkey, yu supposed to be dead, Sparkey.

Heather   No one's laughing.

Bernice   But yu remember don't yu, wat we did. Ca' yu si Clarkey tink I am a fool, a fraud, wasting mi time, on foolishness, but yu were there sister, yu saw wat I did. Tell him.

Heather   I did. Yu did. We told everyone, but no one believed us. Jesus Christ, what is the matter with yu? Clarkey, deal wid her please.

Clarkey   Inside Bernice.

Bernice   I'm not drinkin' yer tea!

Clarkey   Yu hear mi ask yu to?

Bernice   Let go a' me.

Clarkey   Wat de hell mi do now?

Bernice   Is wat yu say to Miss Sandford?

Clarkey   I nuh say nuttin to her.

Bernice   So why she come up to mi in the street, to mi face, say how she glad she get her money back, da mi should not promise wat mi can't deliver. Wat yu do?

Clarkey   Mi pay off one a' yer debts , and dis de tanks I get.

Bernice   Is who tell yu to run my life?

Clarkey   Yu call dis a life?

Bernice   It mine.

Clarkey   Header, listen to wat yer fool of a sister go do.

Bernice   I no fool.

Clarkey   Miss Sandford lose her daughter two year ago, right? Den las' month, Bernice go budda de woman, day and night, tell how she say she get message from the daughter on de oder side.

Bernice   It happened.

Clarkey   Yer fart!

Bernice   Jus' ca' yu nuh si it, it don't mean it never 'appened.

Clarkey   So she tek her money, den she tell de woman, she lose her daughter.

Bernice   Dat 'appens as well.

Clarkey   And she spend all she money.

Bernice   De daughter come back, Clarkey.

Clarkey (*laughs*)   When?

Bernice   Yu tink Miss Sandford go believe mi now?

Clarkey   No one do.

Bernice *throws her bottle at him.*

Heather   Stop it.

Bernice   Gwan, laugh 'bout dat now. Gwan! Yu still love mi now Clarkey?

Clarkey   Yu want fer mi to say no, don't it? Yu want end dis, yu tell mi to my face. I si yu Header. (*Exits.*)

Heather   You always love to hurt that man. One day he won't come back.

Bernice   Clarkey a ball, yu throw 'im against a wall, 'im aways come back.

Heather   Don't be so sure.

Bernice   Still like him, right?

Heather   No.

Bernice   Yu used to.

Heather   When I was twelve.

Bernice   Marry him if yu want.

Heather   Go to bed.

Bernice   Yu look after him mudda. De old bitch.

Heather   Look Berni . . . Mother? Are you telling me that woman is still alive?

Bernice   He nuh mention her?

Heather   No. I jus' assumed she was dead. Bloody hell, Mrs Clark! How old is she now?

Bernice   I don't blasted know. A hundred or summin.

Heather   Even when we were little girls, she was still an old woman.

Bernice   She jus' won't die de old cow! And she miserable, Jesus! 'When yu go marry mi bwoy, yu farm de fool too much Bernice Stuart. Come like yer mudda. Is why yu nuh drink mi tea?' I'm sure she stayin' alive jus' to spite mi, yu nuh. Everytime I'm round deh, I love to slam all de doors real hard. I hope it give her a shock, mek she fall down dead from her heart, but nuh, she still deh.

Heather   It's not his fault he has a mother like that.

Bernice   Mi know.

Heather   So what are you waiting for? Marry him.

Bernice   Header, do yu really tink I would ever let any old bitch like she come between mi and a man I love from de bottom of my heart?

Heather   You have got to tell him.

Bernice   How can I wid him puppy eyes?

Heather   He's not a dog. Tell him the truth if that's how you really feel . . .

Bernice   Oh so it yu dat turn into my mudda now.

Heather   Fine, you carry on, talk to your ghosts for the rest of your life.

Bernice   Well, we can't all be doctor.

Heather   You could have been anything you want. Clarkey was only trying to help you.

Bernice   Oh yu go mek mi cry.

Heather   He loves you, Bernice. God knows why. I've never seen a man so desperate to live with somebody.

Bernice   Dat'll suit yu won't it? Mi wid Clarkey so yu can have de house to yerself, right?

Heather   I am not interested in the bloody house.

Bernice   Why 'im leave de house to yu? Yu five thousand miles away, an' 'im give it to yu.

Heather   Don't blame me because you wasted half yer life looking after him.

Bernice   Clive Stuart loved me.

Heather   Clive Stuart loved Clive Stuart.

Bernice   Yu were jealous!

Heather   Jealous a' wat! You're just another one of his kids he's got scattered all over the planet. 'Bout mi jealous. He was a loser. Go buy yourself another bottle.

Bernice   Look 'pon she, 'im favourite daughter, when yu come back here fer 'im funeral, lording it up all up, flashing she money, Doctor Heather Mackenzie act like she better dan we. No lightning go strike her, she lucky. Different story now aint it? (*Realises what she's said.*) Mi nuh mean dat.

Heather   You did.

Bernice   It de drink dat talk.

Heather   It's yer voice mi hear.

Janet *enters, looking absolutely terrified.*

Heather   Janet? Janet wat is wrong with you?

Janet   Andy . . . Andy . . .

Heather   What . . . what are you talking about?

Janet *struggles to get the words out.*

Heather   Janet!

Janet   Andy.

Heather   What about him?

Janet *sneezes.*

Heather   Oh God.

Bernice   Janet, wat is wrong child, yu look like yu si a ghost. (*Clocks* **Janet***'s expression.*) Janet?

Janet *laughs out loud.*

Heather   You are going insane young lady.

Bernice   Can't yu si she upset about summin . . .

Heather   . . . She's makin' a fool of herself. Janet, go inside before you sneeze yerself to death.

Janet *lets out a scream in anger.*

Heather   Look at you!

Janet *screams again, right in front of her mother's face.* **Heather** *replies with a slap across the head.*

Bernice   Header!

Janet *runs inside.*

Bernice   Wa' wrong wid yu? Summin was troubling her.

Heather   Summin is aways troubling her. She got troubles coming out of her arse.

Bernice   Yu couldn't find out wat was wrong? Yu had to slap her down like dat?

Heather   Yu don't know, Bernice.

Bernice   Know wat, Header?

Heather   Yer right yer nuh, all this, completely different story.

Bernice   I didn't mean dat. Header?

Heather   Bring him to me.

Bernice   Wat?

Heather   Yu done it before. With Sparkey. Bring my boy back to me, Bernice.

Bernice   So it's now yu believe mi?

Heather   Look at her, thirty-two years of my life. Thass all I have to show for. I want my son back. Please.

Scene Six

Outside **Bernice***'s house.* **Clarkey** *is with* **Bernice**.

Clarkey   ARE YU OUTTA YER BLASTED MIND?

Bernice   Mi knew mi shouldn't have tell yu.

Clarkey   I never hear anyting more stupid in my entire life.

Bernice   Clarkey I can do dis.

Clarkey   Is dis yer way a mekin' yer daddy love yu?

Bernice   She need mi Clarkey, fer de first time in her life, she need mi. I sick an' tired a' everybody pushin' mi aside, all mi life, well no more.

Clarkey   Yu ever si mi do dat to yu?

Bernice   Yu never believed in wat I can do, not fer a second.

Clarkey   Yu comin' home wid mi right now yu understand? Stop farmin de arse wid yerself woman!

Bernice *laughs.*

Clarkey   Stop dat, yu love to mek fun a' mi.

Bernice   Is ware yu learn to act so big?

Clarkey   Mama aways said yu want tekin' in hand . . .

Bernice   Yer mudda talk shit. Yu wan' leave her, and dat so-called son a' yours.

Clarkey   Deh my family.

Bernice   I know. So go home. Clarkey go home man.

Clarkey No! I wan' si yu do dis. I want si yu standing in de middle a dat grave and talk to dat bwoy, mi wan' si yu talk. Yu say I never believe yu, prove mi wrong den. Come!

Bernice How de hell yu expect mi to do anyting wid yu standin' deh?

Clarkey Nuh mek excuse.

Bernice I nuh mek excuse. My mind need to be clear, of all thoughts, except dem of de spirits.

Clarkey A' course.

Bernice Yu si? Dat exactly wat mi talking about. How de hell can I manage to do anyting, wid yu aways deh.

Clarkey Yu blamin' mi?

Bernice Yer aways in my way.

Clarkey But yu can't do it.

Bernice Clarkey yu have to stop dis awright. Yu know yu do. Mi nuh love yu.

Clarkey Shut up.

Bernice It trut'.

Clarkey Yu mad?

Bernice Clarkey?

Clarkey Yu wan' lie down, yu nuh feel well.

Bernice I tellin' yu, to yer face! I bin feelin' like dis fer years man, but yu too stupid to listen.

Clarkey Is why yu say dis fer?

Bernice Yu an' mi more like brudda an' sister, it nuh right, it nuh feel right.

Clarkey It feel right to mi. Why yu want dash 'way wat we have?

Bernice Ca' it trut', hear mi please!

Clarkey   So wat mi do now?

Bernice   Marry Junie Riley, mi nuh know.

Clarkey   Yu nuh care.

Bernice   Right!

Clarkey   Truth finally leave yer mout'.

Bernice   Mi never want fer hurt yu Clarkey.

Clarkey (*snaps*)   No budda wid dat!

Bernice   I try . . .

Clarkey   Yu nuh try, yu gwan on about love, yu can't even si love when it right under yer nose. Yu carry on wid yer spirit dem.

Bernice   Tek care a' yerself Clarkey.

Clarkey   Yu wan' follow yer own advice.

Scene Seven

Graveside.

Janet *is alone with her brother.*

Janet (*laughing*)   No! No it was yu! Don't lie Andy. I distracted Mum, yu were the one who unscrewed the top of the salt bottle, and I dared yu to, cos it was my turn to dare yu remember? Shame! The look on her face, remember that? I thought she was gonna croak man. The salt went all over her chips. And as usual she looked at me like I was the one who did it. Like butter wouldn't melt in yer mouth. You were her favourite, you know yu were. Who she give the belt to? Thank yu. (*Mocks.*) Yu got licks, yu got shit. I'm jus' stating a fact thass all. (*Aside.*) Virgin! Sorry. (*Aside.*) Short arse. Yer dead and yu still can't take a joke. Andy hold up, hold up man. I wanna ask yu summin? Can I, yu know, touch yu?

Janet *reaches out for her brother's hand.*

Janet   Am I doing it, am I touchin' yer? Oh man this is weird. Yu know yu really scared me the oder day yu bastard. Yu tryin' to kill me or wat, yu want me lined up next to yu or summin? Why me? Why not Mum? She loves yu, she doesn't love me. (*She listens.*) I can't tell her that. I can't tell her that. It was your fault. Kiss my arse, I aint doin' it. Wat chance? Wat bloody chance could I have wid her?

Heather *and* **Bernice** *enter.*

Heather   This has to work.

Bernice   It'll work.

Janet   Will wat work?

Heather   What are you doing here?

Janet   Nuttin special. Wat yu doin'?

Heather   Nothing.

Janet   Come on.

Heather   It does not concern you. Come let's go Bernice.

Bernice *walks around the field.*

Heather   Bernice?

Janet   What's goin' on here Mum?

Heather   Shush! Bernice?

Bernice *senses something.*

Heather   What, what is it?

Bernice   Deh's sum troubled spirits here man.

Heather   Andrew?

Janet   Andy?

Heather   Where is he? Let me talk to him.

Bernice   Hold on, mi never say it were Andy.

Heather   Who den?

Bernice   Jus' spirits. Dem don' run up an' tell mi who deh are yu nuh, it tek time first. Deh wan' fer know if I can be trusted.

Heather   Well hurry up and say yes.

Bernice   Ease up nuh!

Janet   Yu trying to speak to Andy?

Bernice   Maybe, why?

Janet   Nuttin.

Bernice *walks around the graveyard with eyes closed tight.* **Heather** *follows her.*

Heather   Bernice? Andrew? Andrew, yu there boy?

Bernice   Quiet!

Heather   It's yer mother.

Bernice   Yu want mi to do dis or not?

Heather   Of course I do.

Bernice   Den shut up. Yu'll scare dem.

Heather   Jus' get him.

Bernice   I'm tryin'. Andrew? Andrew? Yu deh bwoy? (*Pretends she can sense something.*)

Heather   Wat is it?

Bernice   Shush.

Janet   Wat she say?

Heather   Shush!

Janet   I only asked.

Heather   Janet! Sorry Bernice.

Bernice   Someone's here. I can feel dem.

Janet   Who?

Bernice   Andrew! Is dat yu bwoy?

Heather   I want to talk to him.

Bernice   Ware yu bin?

Heather   Let me speak to him.

Bernice   Yer mama here Andrew, she want talk to yu, yu ready?

Heather   Where is he?

Bernice   'Im right here, right here in front a' yu.

Janet   Wat?

Heather   Oh God! Andrew? How you doing son?

Janet   Mum?

Bernice   He misses you.

Heather   Oh darling I miss you too.

Bernice   'Im standing right beside yu now.

Janet   Mum!

Bernice   'Im get so big! 'Im right there, Header.

Heather *closes her eyes and imagines she can feel touching her son's face.*

Janet   Mum listen to me.

Heather   Move!

Janet   Listen.

Bernice (*grabs* **Janet***'s arm*)   Wat yu think yer doing?

Janet   Wat do yu think yer doing?

Bernice   She get her son back.

Janet   Oh really? Yu are sick!

Bernice   Watch yer mout' gal.

Janet   Don't threaten me.

Heather   My boy.

Janet (*slaps* **Heather**'s *hands down*)   Yer boy isn't there, Mum.

Heather   What yu doing?

Janet   All yer touching is air!

Heather   Look if you don't believe that is up to you.

Janet   But I do.

Bernice   Go away child.

Heather   Right now.

Janet   Andy is here, Mum, but he's talking to me not her.

Bernice   Yu have de gift?

Heather   Janet! Don't do this to me.

Janet   Doin' wat? I aint hurtin' yu, I've never meant to hurt yu.

Heather   Andrew, yu still here? Yu still here boy?

Janet   'You are going back to college, young man. I don't know what you have to do to grow some sense back into your head, but you had better do it, and you'd better do it now!'

Heather (*stunned*)   Wat?

Janet   It was the last thing you said to him weren't it? He just told me to say it Mum. (*Relaying.*) Your pager went off, some emergency at the hospital. Andy swore at you, then he stormed out of the house. He just told me, he's telling me. Thass wat happened the last time you saw him alive.

Heather   He told you before he died.

Janet   Mum, I'm not lying.

Heather (*confused*)   What the hell is going on here?

Bernice   Header come on!

Janet   She's lying, I'm telling the truth, I swear to yu. Get her to ask Andy summin, summin only yu two would know. Do it, Mum. Trust me for once in yer life, ask her right now! I know yu've aways hated me, Mum, I've felt it all my life, so wat am I doin here? I got no reason to help yu, will yu ask her!

Heather   Bernice?

Bernice   Yu come to mi right, yu come and yu beg.

Heather   Ask him . . .

Bernice (*cuts her off*)   No!

Heather   You ask him where he spent his fifteenth birthday.

Bernice   Yu tink him go remember that?

Heather   He'll remember.

Bernice   Woman come to mi right, on her hands and knees . . .

Heather   Are you going to ask him or not?

Bernice   'Bring my boy back to mi Bernice!'

Heather   You can't do it. He spent the night in hospital, he had food poisoning, I stayed up all night with him, he was so scared. I could kill you.

Bernice (*laughs*)   Woman love to moan eeh? I give her wat she want.

Heather   I wanted my son.

Bernice   I gave yu wat yu needed, to believe.

Heather   I'm selling the house. You hear me Bernice, I'm going to throw you out on the bloody street. One thing I ask you to do for me!

Bernice   So why yu ask mi fer? Yu so good, yu so perfect, yu nuh mek mistake.

Heather   Yu really want to hurt me.

Bernice   Yu hurt yerself. Least Daddy have de strength to know 'im mek a mistake.

Heather   Don't compare me to him.

Bernice   So wat yu doin' here, Header? Wat yu need mi fer?

Heather   I didn't fail my son, right? And I want him to tell me that, Bernice, I need him to tell me.

Janet   Yu didn't fail him, Mum. But he was thinking of quitting college though.

Heather   No!

Janet   He jus' told me.

Heather   No! He was winding me up, Janet, you know what he was like. Isn't that true, son? Tell her.

Janet   No Mum . . .

Heather   You think I don't know my son, Janet? My child? You think I didn't know about those stupid games he played just to get attention? You were just teasing me, Andrew, you were joking. Come on boy! Talk to me.

Janet   He didn't want to fight yu.

Heather   I don't want to hear another word. Why would Andrew contact you?

Janet   I don't know.

Heather   Yu were always jealous of him.

Janet   Oh it really sticks in your throat don't it? That he's talking to me not yu, yer precious little boy.

Heather   You're just like your father Janet, you're weak.

Janet   Fuck yu both! (*Exits.*)

Bernice (*laughs to herself*)   Oh yes, Header no mek mistake.

Heather (*pleads*)   Andrew!

Bernice   Yu know when yu first go to England, dat night I pray fer yer plane to crash, yu nuh, right slam into de ocean. An' when yu get deh, I pray dat yu fall down sick, or get lick down by a car. I pray fer anyting that could 'appen to yu. Cos maybe den right, my daddy would remember 'im have anudda daughter.

Heather *laughs.*

Bernice   Yu tink I mek joke?

Heather   He weren't the same daddy. Soon after we step off the plane, we're walking through the terminal, I'm holding Mama's hand, she look so good, so thin, she was beautiful. Then we see this rough-looking man walking towards us, I ask 'Who is dat?' Mama say 'Das yer daddy.' 'Nuh' I say, 'dat not mi daddy, ware 'im gold tooth, ware 'im smile. Mi nuh want dat. Mi want mi daddy.'

Bernice   I wanted yu dead.

Heather   I wanted to die.

Scene Eight

Outside **Bernice**'s *house. The distraught* **Janet** *is talking with Andy.*

Janet   FUCK HER. FUCK HER, FUCK HER, FUCK HER. I do mean it. Don't tell me how I feel, I hate her, listen to me, hear the words comin' outta my mouth, I hate her. No, I don't know wat yer chattin' about, leave me, I told yu before, no. Yu've never helped me in yer life, why yu stressin' me? I can't man.

Scene Nine

The graveyard.

Bernice *is alone and drunk.*

Bernice   Daddy! Oh Daddy! Yu hear mi Daddy ware yu deh? Are yu here? Or, are yu over deh! Nuh, man, yu over here, yes, yer standin' right beside mi, yes. (*Holds out her hand.*) Yu holdin' mi hand, yer daughter's hand? Yu kissin' yer lovely daughter's hand, Daddy? Daddy? Yer lovely daughter, Daddy, de one who tek care a' yu? Is Mama wid yu? Yu tell her I doin' fine right, Bernice is doin' fine! Mi had a whole heap of spirits come visit mi, yessir. Ca' dem got unfinished business in this world like Mama used to say, ca' dem loved ones want chat to dem. I is providing a service, Bernice Stuart, spiritualist advisor. Yu like de sound a' dat Daddy? No, course yu don't. Yu don't. A whole heap of spirits want talk to mi Daddy, but not yu, nossir! But yu go have to help mi now Daddy, ca' dem spirits gone, long time deh nuh talk. And I wan' fer dem to talk, oderwise mi got no life. Yu want fer dat to happen. Help mi, gwan shake up dem spirits, Daddy, tell dem to get deh backsides down here, tell dem mi not so bad, mi can help dem. Or better yet, yu come down, come talk to mi, yer daughter. Daddy? I bet if mi name was Header, yu'd come down, yu'd rush down. Not even God could stop yu. If yu love her so much, is why yu come back, is why yu leff her in England, why yu nuh stay deh? Is why yu never tell mi de one thing I wanted to hear all mi life.

Janet (*enters*)   Go away!

Bernice   Janet?

Janet   Piss off!

Bernice   Is who dat budda yu?

Janet   This fool, he won't go leave me, I got nuttin more to say to yu right!

Bernice   Si dem spirits want talk to yu now, Janet.

Janet   It's only one.

Bernice   Don't worry. Soon dem all come.

Janet   I don't want them to.

Bernice (*laughs at the irony*)   Yu don't want them to? (*Yells.*) SHE DON'T WANT DEM TO!

Janet   Help me, Auntie.

Bernice   Child I can't.

Janet   Please jus' get rid of him for me.

Bernice   I CAN'T! But yu can help mi, right? Yeah, yeah yu help mi. Speak to yer granddaddy fer mi, yu tell 'im right, yu tell 'im dat he aint nuttin but an old bastard right, and him foot stink! Deh stink! Tell him all de time I had to tek off dem man's shoes so I can put him to bed I hold mi nose in case it fall off, ca' him foot stink, right? Real bad. Yu tell him, Janet, yu go tell him.

Janet   I don't want it. Yu have it.

Bernice   If yer brudda still here right, den it ca' 'im still have business to do, an 'im walking round till it get done.

Janet (*to Andy*)   I hate yu!

Bernice   Dat nuh go mek 'im go. Yu have to mek tings right. Mi can't help yu.

Heather *enters.*

Bernice (*sees* **Heather**)   Lord I can't even get drunk in peace! (*Exits.*)

Heather *kneels by the grave to change the flowers.*

Janet   Am I that much of a disappointment to yu, Mum?

Heather   You had every chance he had.

Janet   Thass a laugh.

Heather   You threw it away.

Janet   So I wasn't as smart as Andy was, is that a crime?

Heather   I didn't raise my children to sit on their arses.

Janet   Oh man.

Heather   Wid a cup in their hands. You are more than what they tell you child.

Janet   Same old shit, all my life. Let me become what I wanna be.

Heather   A drifter.

Janet   My business.

Heather   What are you going to drift into next, Janet, after you and your boyfriend have run your restaurant into the ground?

Janet   Ryan! RY-AN. I swear to God, Mum, yer gonna say his name one day. Why yu want to see me fail?

Heather   Why do you? You were only sixteen, Janet.

Janet   Don't!

Heather   Sixteen! And you threw away your life. And for what? To get yourself a good fuck? An excuse for him to tell his friends, 'Yeah man, yu shoulda seen me bredren, yessir, I was givin' her sum serious portions.'

Janet *laughs*.

Heather   Yeah it's funny, Janet.

Janet   I don't think I've heard yu swear. Serious portions? Ryan weren't like that. We loved each other, we still do. Yu don't know us. I don't need yer acceptance no more.

Heather   Fine then, go home.

Janet   Yu go, I aint running from yu, it's wat Andy did.
Yu jus' wouldn't see how badly he needed to get away from
yu.

Heather   All I wanted wat was best for him.

Janet   Best for who though? Every day, man, yu were
pushin' him. Yu didn't raise a son, yu raised a
schizophrenic. He pretended he could handle everything yu
wanted for him, but inside he was crackin'.

Heather   Yu leave him alone, right?

Janet   Yu wanna know about him sneakin' into my
room . . .

Heather   Leave him!

Janet   . . . going through my drawers, readin' my diary,
thass how he knew I was pregnant, an' he couldn't wait to
tell yu, he didn't have the guts to front yu up about his
problems, so he took it out on me, ennit broth?

Heather   This child love to lie!

Janet   Mum, yu gotta listen to me, right? He was so
wound up, up for fighting anyone he was. Desperate to
prove to himself, jus' once, that he could be someone else.
Andy started the fight.

Heather   No.

Janet   I was there, Mum. I saw wat 'appened.

Heather   Wat yu mean yu saw? Yu said yu found him
lying there.

Janet   I know wat I said, I lied.

Heather   Oh God.

Janet   Everything that guy said in court was true, it was
self defence, Andy woulda killed Nicholls. He didn't know
who he was.

Heather　No. Child love to lie.

Janet　Mum let go of him. Jus' do it.

Heather　And then what?

Janet　Bloody hell! Did I always look wrong to yu? Was I born one minute and yu told the doctor 'Errgh, I don't want that, take it!' Is that how it was? Yu think I deserve it, yu don't think I hate myself?

Heather　Good. Yu should. Going on all the time about yu doin' nuttin wrong, that you didn't love to annoy me, going out wid that boy. (*Cuts in before* **Janet** *can.*) RY-AN! When you should have been at school. Andrew? So, is this the thanks I get? Andrew? Boy yu better answer me when I speak to yu! (*She waits.*) Yu nuh answer? Huh? Well you can go to hell boy. (*To* **Janet**.) Are you happy now?

Janet　No.

Heather　Child love to lie.

Janet　He knows yu don't mean it. He says he's standing next to yu.

Heather *moves away.*

Janet　Wat yu doin'? Ware yu goin'?

Heather　I'm lettin' go.

Janet　Yu don't want to say goodbye first?

Heather　If he's goin', he's goin', but tell him to go now. He gone yet?

Janet　I can't hear him.

Heather　He gone yet?

Janet　Yes.

Heather　Come let's go.

Janet　Mum?

Heather Wat?

Janet Wat about us?

Scene Ten

Outside **Bernice**'s *house. Bernice is with* **Clarkey** *who is lifting her up in the air, swinging her around in the yard.*

Clarkey (*thrilled*)   Oh yes, yeah man!

Bernice Yu want put mi down before yu hurt yer back!

Clarkey Bernice! Yu love to give man hard time, yu nuh.

Bernice I said yes.

Clarkey Mi know, mi know. It were my mudda right, she dat mek yu 'fraid, right?

Bernice Right.

Clarkey All yu had to do were tell mi.

Bernice Awright man.

Clarkey Sorry, sorry. But yu nuh have to worry 'bout dat no more right. Yu go be de woman of de house, Mama go have to do wat yu say.

Bernice She go obey mi?

Clarkey Yes! And if she nuh like it, it too bad. And if dat son a' mine give yu trouble, yu tell mi and I go lick off 'im head. Wat kinda ring yu want?

Bernice I don't mind. Long as it nuh cheap.

Clarkey Mama say yu can wear her wedding dress.

Bernice I nuh go wear her old dress.

Clarkey It look nice Bernice, she tek care good care a' it.

Bernice   I don't care. I wan' be wearing a brand new dress from de shop, right? Yer mama dress! Yu best get dat money yu got hidin' under yer bed.

Clarkey   Shush.

Bernice   Clarkey! Yu don't really keep it under yer bed, man?

Clarkey   We go be happy.

Janet *comes out of the house, followed by* **Heather**.

Heather (*holding up a packet of tissues*)   You forgot these.

Janet   Cheers.

Heather   Don't want yu sneezing all the way home. You're going be late you know.

Clarkey   Hey Header, guess what . . .

Bernice   We bump into yer old boyfriend today, Georgie Taylor! 'Im tell us to say how'd yu do and 'im say 'im go come round soon.

Clarkey (*confused*)   Wa gwan?

Bernice   Yu go miss de plane.

Clarkey   Come Janet. (*Exits.*)

Janet *kisses* **Heather** *on the cheek, smiles.*

Heather   Wat?

Janet   Yu got my lipstick on yer cheek. Here.

Janet *uses one of her tissues to wipe the lipstick off* **Heather**'s *cheek.*

Heather   Call me when you get home, yeah?

Janet (*nods*)   Keep an eye on her for me, Auntie.

Heather   Keep an eye on me? You keep an eye on yourself, child.

Car horn beeps.

Janet   Laters. (*Exits.*)

Bernice   Alone at last, hey?

Heather   Fine. (*Hands her a letter.*)

Bernice   Wat dis?

Heather   Deeds to the house. It's yours.

Bernice   It's now yu realise?

Heather   Tek it nuh.

Bernice   No.

Heather   Wat yu mean, no?

Bernice   Mi mean no, mi nuh wan' it. Yu dat Daddy leave it to.

Heather   It's now yu realise? Take the house, Bernice.

Bernice   Mi nuh want it, Header.

Heather   I don't want it either.

Bernice   Too bad.

Heather   Well what are you going to do?

Bernice   Go live wid Clarkey.

Heather   Yu don't love him.

Bernice   Mi go marry him.

Heather   What?

Bernice   Yu deaf?

Heather   Yu mad!

Bernice   Yu say I should.

Heather   And it's now you start listening to me? Yu go marry a man yu don't love?

Bernice   'Im love mi. Dat'll do. Is why yu love to mek tings so complicated fer?

Heather   Never mind.

Bernice   Good, keep yer nose out.

Heather   So what do I do with the house?

Bernice   Leff it, burn it, I don't care any more!

Heather   Alright. (*Laughs.*)

Bernice   Wat yu laugh at?

Heather   Georgie Taylor? He's the one who had slick black hair, right? Wid 'im Tony Curtis look. 'Im drive a fancy car.

Bernice   An 'im have a fit behind.

Heather   Yes I remember him.

Bernice   Yu wan' drop by and say hello? Mi know ware 'im live.

Heather   No!

Bernice   Oh Header, don't be so . . . english!

Heather   No.

Bernice   Slip yu?

Heather *shakes her head.*

Bernice   Slip yu! (*Tags her, then runs off.*)

Heather   I'm not coming.

Bernice (*off*)   Come on, Header.

Heather *goes to run off stage, following after her sister. She feels a wind coming up behind her. She decides to make one last attempt.*

Heather   Son?

Bernice (*off*)   Header?

Heather *exits.*

Blackout.

Clubland

Act One

Scene One

Palais nightclub (Eighties night).

Kenny *and* **Ben** *come out of the gents loo. They stand and drool by the fruit machine as they watch girls coming out of the ladies. Music is heard in the background. They both start singing along, making up their own lyric to the song that is being played over. They are both drunk.*

Ben   . . . get down on it . . .

Kenny   . . . suck my helmet . . .

Ben   . . . please don't bite it . . .

Together   . . . juss excite it! (*Louder.*) . . . get down on it, suck my helmet, please don't bite it, juss excite it!

Boys laugh. Another pop song plays.

Ben   I don't know the lines to this one. Tell the guy to play Adam and the Ants or summin.

Kenny   Yu tell him. Eighties night is gettin shit.

Ben   Pussy round the clock!

Kenny   They ain't all that.

Ben   Get on the floor and do sum moves. (*Pushes him.*)

Kenny   I ain't dancin to this. There ain't no one on the floor. Except that African and dem girls over there. Look at the prat.

Ben   He's getting amongst it.

Kenny   He's so black he's blue.

Ben   He's getting started.

Kenny   Right sooty.

Ben   Kenny, will yu please get yer arse on the dance floor and show them how it's done.

Kenny   I got all night.

Ben   They're gonna get taken if yu don't move now.

Kenny   Yu go. Yu wanted to come here, I wanted to go up West.

Ben   We always come here.

Kenny   Look how's he's going for them.

Ben   I know.

Kenny   Could he be any more obvious?

Ben   He's having fun.

Kenny   He calls that dancing?

Ben   I don't see them complaining.

Kenny   How old yu reckon?

Ben   Ate een.

Kenny   Wat dog years? (*Presses collect button.*)

Ben   Why yu do that?

Kenny   Saving yer money.

Ben   Yer name Denise? (**Kenny** *taps him on the cheek.*) Get off.

Kenny   Rang Nathan the other day.

Ben   So?

Kenny   Left a message. Melanie musta had the baby by now.

Ben (*so not interested*)   Triffic.

Kenny (*points at sooty*)   Yu really reckon I'm a better dancer than him?

Ben   Look, juss go up and dance near them, show dem yer moves, catch their eyes and that. Go on.

Kenny   Patience, boy, I know wat I'm doin. Yu juss go play wid yer cherries. (*Sees something.*) Oh my God! (*Nudges* **Ben**.)

Ben   Wat!

Kenny *points to* **Ade** *(sooty) who enters. The boys continue to stare at him as he approaches the loo door.* **Kenny** *whispers something to* **Ben**.

Ade   Yeah?

Ben   Ade Boateng, ennit.

Ade   Do I know yu?

Ben   Manor House School.

Ade   Name would help.

Ben   Ben Harper.

Ade   Stevie's brother!

Ben   Yeah, man.

Ade   Awright, man, how's tricks?

Ben   Awright.

Ade   Who's yer friend?

Kenny   Kenny Taylor. Remember me?

Ade   Vaguely.

Ben   Doing awright?

Ade   This and that.

Ben   Yeah, I can see this and that from here.

Ade   Come early yu get the best ones, ennit.

Ben   Damn, man, how yu get so big?

Ade   Few hours down the gym, press-ups. Thirty a day, every day.

Ben   Thass a how yu get the six pack?

Ade   Come wid me, get yu off dem kebabs.

Ben (*prods* **Ade***'s chest*)   No fat, not an inch. Kenny yu gotta touch this come.

Kenny   Get off. (**Ben** *drops to the floor.*) Wat yu doin?

Ben   Like this, Ade?

Ade   Spread yer legs a bit. Now push. Harder.

Kenny   Get up.

The best **Ben** *can manage is four press-ups. He sits up, sweating.*

Ade   Is that the best yu can do?

Ben   I'm fucked.

Ade   I know a guy once, couldn't do more than five press-ups without sweating, had a heart attack when he was thirty, kill him.

Ben   Yu joke?

Ben *puts his beer away. He tries to take* **Kenny***'s bottle off him.*

Kenny   Get off me.

Ben   Yu wanna die before yer thirty?

Kenny   Yu wanna act like a sheep gwan, move yerself.

Ade   I see yer later, girls.

Ben   Ade, hold up, man. Don't suppose yu could see yer way thru lettin us in on sum of the action, yu nuh. I mean yu ain't gonna have all three a' dem.

Ade   I could if I wanted to. Tell yu wat, gimme a minute, then come over.

Kenny   Wat about Denise?

Ade Who?

Kenny He's married.

Ben Love to open yer mout, ennit.

Kenny Kiss my arse.

Ben Suck my dick.

Ade Guys! Wass 'appenin?

Ben We're coming.

Ade One second yeah. (*Exits.*)

Ben Yeah, man! Yu ready?

Kenny Vaguely knows me my arse. Fool only sat next to me in class.

Ben I can't believe thass him.

Kenny Wat is yer name?

Ben He was so skinny.

Kenny Kunta, Kunta Kinte! (*Pretends to crack a whip.*) Yer name is Toby! Kunta Kinte! (*Laughs.*) Remember that?

Ben Say that to his face now. I dare yu.

Kenny Yu think I won't? I ain't kissin his arse like yu. All that press-up shit, wat was all that about?

Ade *comes back out.*

Ade Awright, come. (*Leaves.*)

Ben Come.

Kenny Ware yu goin? Let's juss wait.

Ben I don't wanna wait.

Kenny Yu tellin me yu want hang round wid Ade Boateng?

Ben I wanna enjoy myself.

Kenny   Awright, let's go.

Ben   Don't gimme no grief, man.

Kenny   Shut up.

Ben   No dropping of Denise into the conversation.

Kenny   Yu mean yer wife.

Ben   See thass the shit I'm talking about.

Kenny   I won't.

Ben   Yu might get a bit too, yer nuh. Juss don't do yer pussy act.

Kenny   Is who yu callin pussy?

Scene Two

Sandra's *living room.*

Ade *is trying to watch tele.* **Sandra** *is chatting away on her mobile.*

Sandra   . . . cos he's a fuckin bastard thass why! I mean who the fuck does he think he is? He ain't nuttin! The second I fuckin lay eye on him right, I told the girl I say 'Nicole, Nicole, darlin, that Brendan of yours ain't nuttin, he ain't worth shit, he's a fuckin crackhead, drop him.' But nuh she comes back wid, 'Nuh nuh, Sandra, he ain't like that, yu don't know him like I do!' She find out now though ennit, she fuckin know wid her empty purse, empty bank account, empty flat. He fleeced her good, TV, video, radio, anything that wasn't nailed down, he even fuckin teif her little kid's playstation man, juss so that he can buy his fuckin shit and get fuckin high. Hear how she try tellin me it was a burglary and Brendan had nuttin to do wid it. Carryin on like I got stupid written on my fuckin forehead.

Ade *tries to get into the movie, but gives up, he turns it off with the remote.* **Ade** *looks away clearly disgusted by* **Sandra**'s *language.*

Sandra   He is lucky he didn't do that in front of me, he is fuckin lucky. Cos I woulda killed him, Sonya, on the Bible I fuckin swear to yu, I woulda killed the cunt! Yu know summin, God forgive me yeah, but I hope he teifs from her again, I hope he teifs from her kid, from her mum, from everybody she knows, robs dem fuckin blind, and I hope I'm there when he does it, I walk right in and catch him in the middle of it, it'll be worth it, Sonya, cos then fuckin watch me, I'll juss pick up the first thing that comes into view, I don't care wat it is, telephone, microwave, a fuckin hammer, I'll bury it into the fucker's head! Then I'll stand over the fucker, watch the fucker bleed to death and laugh my fuckin arse off! Oh Sonya, man, yu shouldn't have told me any of this, who the fuck does he think he is! (*Sudden change in mood.*) So anyway, darlin, how yu doin, yu awright? No. No! Oh darlin, thass fuckin brilliant? So when did he ask? And it's now yu tell me? (*Laughs.*) Well, it's about fuckin time, don't yu think? Sonya gettin married, fer fucks sake, wass the world comin to. Whoa, whoa, wat yu mean yu gotta go, this girl makes me laugh, man, yu tell me yer engaged and yu gotta go, sit yer arse down, woman! Yeah yeah, I suppose, yu gotta go then, ennit, go on move then, yu fuckin lightweight. But yu best call me when yu get back, or I'm comin over deh to kick yer sorry black arse, yu get me? We'll have to go out, it's yer birthday soon, ennit? Yeah, yu too, darlin, be good yeah, love yer too. (*Hangs up. Clocks'* **Ade***'s face.*) Yes?

Ade   Did yer mother ever wash yer mouth out with soap?

Sandra   Yeah, but it didn't do any fuckin good. Shouldn't have bin listen.

Ade   Hard not to.

Sandra   Yu should have words wid him.

Ade   I will.

Sandra   Good.

Ade   I'm playin pool wid him later, I'll buy him a card or summin.

Sandra   Not Sonya and Trevor yu fool!

Ade   Who den?

Sandra   Nicole and that fuckin cunt Brendan.

Ade   Do yu have to swear?

Sandra   Yeah, I fuckin do.

Ade   Every time yu do, I feel sick.

Sandra   Well pardon fuckin me.

Ade   Would it kill yer to be a bit more . . .

Sandra   Wat?

Ade   Sensitive.

Sandra   Yer chat is dry.

Ade   I tell yer, man . . .

Sandra   Are yu gonna have words wid him?

Ade   Why?

Sandra   He's outta order.

Ade   How yu know she ain't on crack herself?

Sandra   Say that again?

Ade   Nicole ain't no Pollyanna right.

Sandra   Go screw.

Ade   Juss let 'em get on wid it. One week from now, they'll be huggin and kissin again.

Sandra   Not if I've got anythin to do wid it.

Ade   Wat yu gonna do?

Sandra   Yu'll find out.

Ade   Yu ain't gonna do shit.

Sandra   Bwoy, move.

Ade   Keep yer nose out.

Sandra   Move.

Ade   Will yu stop talkin like that. Yu ain't Nicole. Yer a sarf London girl, Sandra, deal wid it.

Sandra   Yu know a lot about sarf London girls, ennit.

Ade   Sorry?

Sandra   Nuttin.

Ade   Can I watch my film now?

Sandra   Oh wat for?

Ade   Cos it's good.

Sandra   It's shit.

Ade   Wass up, Sandra, too much hard work for yer?

Sandra   I don't know wat was wrong wid *Men in Black*.

Ade   Yu wanna talk about shit.

Sandra   Juss cos I don't go for none of yer foreign crap, who yu tryin to impress this week, Ade?

Ade   Yu see any subtitles on this one?

Sandra   I still don't like it.

Ade   Yu juss can't handle anythin that requires yu to use yer brain. Has to be obvious, no matter how bad.

Sandra   Wat about this one?

Ade   Don't even try.

Sandra   So obvious it's untrue.

Ade   Yer dreamin.

Sandra   It's him, ennit?

Ade   Who?

Sandra   The cripple guy.

Ade   Not necessarily.

Sandra   Bet it is.

Ade   How can yu possibly know that?

Sandra   He's makin the story up. He's tellin that copper wat he wants to hear.

Ade   Yu seen this film, ain't yer?

Sandra   No.

Ade   Don't lie.

Sandra   I ain't lying.

Ade   Yu've bloody seen it.

Sandra   I ain't.

Ade   I really wanted to see this yu know.

Sandra   So watch it.

Ade   How can I when yu juss told me.

Sandra   I might be wrong.

Ade   Yu've seen it, Sandra, I know yu have.

Sandra   I ain't!

Ade   Any time I want to relax.

Sandra   I ain't seen it! (*He ignores her.*) Wass the matter wid yer, didn't score lass night?

Ade   Wat?

Sandra   Yu heard me.

Ade   No.

Sandra   Yu try to?

Ade   No.

Sandra   Yu go up West?

Ade   I didn't score. I got a girl.

Sandra   Don't touch me.

Ade   Yu got summin to say?

Sandra   Ware were yu all night?

Ade   Oh man, do we have to go through this again?

Sandra   Juss answer the question.

Ade   I told yu, playin cards wid Leroy.

Sandra   Yu didn't phone.

Ade   Yu my mum?

Sandra   I was worried.

Ade   I went straight to work, wass yer problem?

Sandra   Watch the film.

Ade   Wat Sandra?

Sandra   I haven't seen it, I swear to yer.

Ade   Wat!

Sandra   Watch the film!

Ade *goes back to watching the movie. He tries to relax back into it but cannot, he notices* **Sandra** *is staring at him.*

Ade   Fucks sake, wat!

Sandra *slowly unbuttons her shirt to reveal her bra.*

Ade *(getting aroused)*   Yeah, now wat?

Sandra   Get the handcuffs. (**Ade** *laughs.*) Ade, don't make me beg.

Ade   Yu said no last time.

Sandra   Girl can't change her mind?

Ade   Yu do on a regular basis.

Sandra   Juss get them.

Ade *jumps up like a little boy about to open his presents. He exits for a brief moment out of the room.* **Sandra** *feels a little cold, nervous even.* **Ade** *returns with a set of handcuffs.* **Sandra** *surrenders her hands without looking at him.* **Ade** *handcuffs her.*

Ade   Don't look so worried.

Ade *gives her a genuine loving kiss. This calms* **Sandra** *a little. Perhaps it will not be so bad she thinks.* **Ade** *positions himself, he unbuckles his belt, ready to take* **Sandra** *from behind.*

Ade   How deep yu want it?

Sandra   Deep.

Ade   Really deep?

Sandra   Yeah, yeah, really deep . . . (*Bursts out laughing.*) Sorry, sorry!

Ade   You don't want to do it, fuckin say so.

Sandra   Language.

Ade   So why tell me to get the handcuffs?

Sandra   I dunno. Maybe cos I'm tryin to understand yu.

Ade   Understand wat?

Sandra   It's wat yu do wid dem, ennit?

Ade   Whose dem?

Sandra   Will yu please get me out of this.

Ade   No.

Sandra   Ade!

Ade   Yu wanted them, yu stay where yu are.

Sandra   They're hurtin my wrists.

Ade   I'm not a mind-reader, Sandra, wat do yu want from me?

Sandra   Yu not fuckin other girls would be nice.

Ade   I'm not.

Sandra   Don't lie to me.

Ade   Sandra . . .

Sandra   Yvonne saw yu.

Ade   Why yu always believe every word that comes out of her mouth?

Sandra   She saw yu comin outta the Palais wid sum silly little white bitch. The fuckin Palais, Ade. Scraping the bottom of the barrel now, don't yu think?

Ade   How she know it was me?

Sandra   Yu muss tink I'm a right arsehole to mek yer lie so obvious.

Ade   Awright, I went to the Palais, I was chattin to sum white bit on the way out one night, is that a crime?

Sandra   Yu weren't juss chattin, Ade.

Ade   She's lyin about that.

Sandra   Lyin about wat?

Ade   Lyin about watever it is she saw me do.

Sandra   Yu fuckin bastard.

Ade   Oh thass it, ennit? One word from Yvonne the mouth, and I'm tried and convicted.

Sandra   Why would she lie?

Ade   Cos she's a dried-up bitch.

Sandra   She's my mate.

Ade   She ain't no mate, it she yu should be watchin, not me, her.

Sandra   Wat yu chattin about?

Ade   Ask her about New Year's Eve.

Sandra   I'm askin yu.

Ade   Yer brother's party. She had me cornered on the stairs, arms all over me, beggin me to take me upstairs. Horny as fuck. Going on about it's bin years since she free it up for a man, but she'll gladly free it up for me, juss me, and only me. I pushed her away, tell her I didn't want to know, she call me black this . . .

Sandra   Bullshit.

Ade   Black that.

Sandra   Yer lying.

Ade   Thass yer friend.

Sandra   Yu juss love to think every gal in sight wants yu.

Ade   It's the truth.

Sandra   Like any sista's gonna demean herself like that for yu.

Ade   Yu are so naive.

Sandra   Yu and yer fuckin white women.

Ade   Least they ain't frigid.

Sandra   Oh so yu callin me frigid now? Yu didn't say nuttin about me bin frigid when we first went out.

Ade   Things change.

Sandra   Yu ain't makin me feel like this.

Ade   Feel wat yu like.

Sandra   Get the fuck outta my flat. Get the fuck outta my flat.

Ade (*grabs his coat and leaves*)   Frigid bitch.

Sandra   Black bastard! Go chase yer white women!

Sandra *tries again to wriggle out of the handcuffs.*

Sandra   Bastard.

Scene Three

Ben's *back garden.*

Late afternoon.

Ben *is on the ground doing press-ups. He tries to do move than four but gives up. He is panting and sweating as he sits back up.* **Ben** *sits in his deckchair, takes in the sun, and drinks his beer. He reaches for his little tin box on the ground, places it on his lap and starts rolling up a spliff. Sound of a dog barking coming from inside.* **Kenny** *comes running out, he shuts the door quickly behind him.*

Ben   Yu took yer time. Yu better have opened the windows in the toilet, man. Yu awright? Ware's yer beer?

Kenny   In there.

Ben   Well, go get it.

Kenny   Yu are aware there's a big bastard of a dog, runnin around yer house.

Ben   Adolf. Cute, ain't he?

Kenny   Nuh Ben, that ain't a word I'd use. Yu mighta warned me yu bought a dog.

Ben   Forgot.

Kenny   Bollocks yu forgot. Yu plannin on tellin yu were sorry, after the cunt ripped my arse off? Yu called yer fucking dog Adolf?

Ben   I bin trainin him to attack blacks. Nuff burglaries round here committed by yu lot.

Kenny   Yu racist wanker.

Ben   True though.

Kenny   Least we don't rape no women.

Ben   Yu bloody do that as well.

Kenny   Not as much as yu.

Ben (*shouts*)   Adolf? Here, boy!

Kenny   Fuck off, Ben.

Ben (*laughs*)   Look at yer, shittin yerself.

Kenny   Adolf? Watcha yer call him that for?

Ben   Good Aryan name!

Kenny   I bet yu've got swastikas and pictures of Hitler hangin on yer wall when I'm not here. (**Ben** *laughs*.) Don't yer?

Ben   We got 'em put up in the spare room.

Kenny   Gimme the spliff.

Ben   Hold up, there's an art to this.

Kenny   Fuck the art, pass it over.

Ben *finishes rolling it up, he lights up, takes a few puffs before handing it over to* **Kenny**. *The lads relax for a minute, enjoying their spliff, drinking their beer. They put on their sunglasses. Dog starts barking.*

Ben   Shut up, yu ain't comin out.

Kenny   Cheers.

Ben   Ain't doin it for yu, they've got a German shepherd next door, he's bin havin it off wid. Horny little bastard. Only got it pregnant. Dogs' owner went all menstral on me, we gotta take summa the pups, our responsibility. (*Dog is howling.*) I didn't even wan' a dog, shut up. Guess who I saw the oder day? That blonde bit from the Palais lass week.

The one whose mate was gettin off wid Ade. She came into the shop, I sold her a pair of trainers.

Kenny   Yer point?

Ben   She was wid her mum. She was shopping for trainers wid her mum. (*Laughing.*)

Kenny   She said she was nineteen.

Ben   Nineteen minus five more like.

Kenny (*disgusted*)   Oh man! Errgh!

Ben   Wat yu crying for, yu didn't do nuttin.

Kenny   Yeah I know but, errgh!

Ben   She was in her school uniform.

Kenny   Errgh!

Ben   It's Ade yu should be worried about. He had his hand right up her mate's skirt, yu see him? She's got sum front though. There she was in the shop, her mum two feet away, standin there in her gymslip, no shame. Coming on to me. Askin about yu. She's up for yer, Kenny, yu coulda had her.

Kenny   Well I'm glad I didn't. Oh man!

Ben   Only reason nuttin happened cos yu were doin yer pussy act.

Kenny   I ain't no pussy right.

Ben   So wat happened?

Kenny   Didn't fancy it. I had a feeling she was a kid.

Ben   Shut up, man, I saw yer, yer tongue was on the floor dread, nuttin happened cos yu were boring the arse off her about yer job. Who gives a fuck about pensions? Yu think she wants to hear that? She was waitin for the jump, man.

Kenny   So wat about yu?

Ben   She weren't my type.

Kenny   Yer full of shit. I prefer women right, not little girls. It's gotta be right. I want it to feel right.

Ben   Don't do a Nathan on me.

Kenny   I'm not doin anything, I'm juss sayin.

Ben   Sayin wat?

Kenny   Don't it make yu tink sumtimes?

Ben   Wat does?

Kenny   Nate. Yu saw the way him and Mel looked at each other.

Ben   Oh man.

Kenny   So how was it for yu when yu first saw Denise then?

Ben   Nice tits. (**Kenny** *shakes his head.*) It was. Awright she made me laugh, we got on, nuttin special. None of this lovey-lovey crap.

Kenny   This is the woman yu married.

Ben   So? Forget Nate. He don't love that girl. He only married it cos he got it pregnant.

Kenny   Shut up.

Ben   It's true.

Kenny   Yu shouldn't say things like that.

Ben   Ask himself if yu don't believe me.

Kenny   I will.

Ben   Do I look as if I care? Now can we stick to the matter in hand please, yu getting a poke.

Kenny   I don't need yer help for that.

Ben   I didn't see yu turnin up yer nose at my help when yu wanted to shag that girl who worked in the shop.

Kenny   Here we go.

Ben   Debbie. Yu borrowed the keys to my car to take her home one night and yu still didn't shag her.

Kenny   She had a boyfriend.

Ben   Funny how she never mentioned no boyfriend to me.

Kenny   She had a boyfriend awright.

Ben   That girl Ade had, she had a boyfriend.

Kenny   How yu know?

Ben   Heard her tell him.

Kenny   So wat?

Ben   Didn't stop Ade though.

Kenny   Don't compare me to him.

Ben   Ooooh!

Kenny   I gotta better taste.

Ben   Yu say so.

Kenny   I do.

Ben   Yu de man.

Kenny   Ennit.

Ben   How long ago was that wid Debbie?

Kenny   Leave it, Ben.

Ben   A year. And how long since yu had it last?

Kenny   Yer askin fer a slap.

Ben   Yer sack mus be bursting. Overflowing, tidal wave!

Kenny   Will yu shut up.

Ben   I gotta get yu layed. I don't care if it's the biggest slag there is.

Kenny   I ain't goin out tonight. And wat about yu, wouldn't Denise like to see a bit more of her husband?

Ben   Denise can kiss my arse.

Kenny   Wass happened now?

Ben   Take yer pick. The way she eats, the way she talks, sleeps, walks. And her teeth, her teeth Kenny.

Kenny   Ain't that noticeable.

Ben   Yer such a liar. She looks like a horse. Yu know wat, I woke up this morning right, I saw her, reading one of her books, mouth wide open wid her bloody teeth, all for the world to see. I was yawning, stretching out my arms an that, I was so tempted to whack her in the side of her mouth wid my elbow, make out it was an accident, didn't see her there, mash up her teeth though, hopefully. I'll be doing her a favour, yu think she's happy looking like that?

Kenny   Yu need help.

Ben   Like I was really gonna do it.

Kenny   Why don't yu juss leave, man?

Ben   And my job too? Her dad's juss made me manager. Four years of shit I took from him to get that.

Kenny   Yu don't love her.

Ben   I married her.

Kenny   Yer point?

Ben   Yer borin me, Kenny.

Kenny   I warned yu not to do it. Like a fool, yu nuh listen to me.

Ben   Rah, hear him chat like a bro now.

Kenny   Fuck off wid that.

Ben   Joke, man!

Kenny   Tryin to help yu.

Ben   So don't help, problem solved. I do wat I please when I please yu get me? So wat time yu comin round tonight?

Kenny   I'm stayin in.

Ben   Oh fer fuck's sake.

Kenny   I'm stayin in.

Ben   Yeah, laters Nathan.

Kenny   Shut it. (*Pauses before opening the door, sound of dog growling.*) Ben?

Ben   Thass my name.

Kenny   I wanna get out.

Ben   I ain't stoppin yer.

Kenny   The dog.

Ben   He don' bite, much.

Kenny   I wanna go home, yer cunt. Awright! I'll come out.

Ben   Nice one.

Kenny   Yu such a kid.

Ben (*goes inside*)   Prince, upstairs, Prince, upstairs. (*Calls.*) Yu can come in now.

Kenny   Prince?

Ben   Did yu really think I'd call my dog Adolf? Kenny, how long yu known me?

Kenny   Yer a dick.

Ben   Yer not lying to me now?

Kenny   No.

Ben   Good, cos I'll send Prince round after yer. Back here at nine.

Kenny   Yes, Masa. (*Exits.*)

Ben   Yer learnin.

Scene Four

Palais nightclub.

Kenny *is standing with* **Ade** *by the fruit machine.* **Ade** *is looking over at some girls, giving them the eye.*

Ade   Yu don't have to be embarrassed.

Kenny   About wat?

Ade   That yu got a hard-on.

Kenny   Excuse me?

Ade   These girls wouldn't be wearing skirts up to their arses if yu couldn't get a hard-on. That is why they are dressed like that, to get yu hard. Check this one, man.

Kenny   I ain't got a hard-on.

Ade   Yu queer?

Kenny   No.

Ade   So wass yer story? Yer in a club, wall to wall wid trim, an yu don't feel nuttin. Yu queer?

Kenny   Awright I've got one.

Ade   Got wat?

Kenny   A hard-on.

Ade (*laughs*)   Go deh.

Kenny   So wat about yu?

Ade   I ain't tellin yu.

Kenny   I juss told yu.

Ade   So?

Kenny   Yu have.

Ade   Maybe.

Kenny   Got the biggest one there is.

Ade   Maybe not.

Kenny   Yer tongue's on the floor.

Ade   Thass my business, I ain't going round tellin people how big my stiffie is. Yer such a fool, Mr Lame. A dog could do better than yu.

Kenny   Mr Lame. Thass wat we used to call yu at school.

Ade   And other things.

Kenny   I knew yu remembered me.

Ade   My first day at school, couldn't speak much English.

Kenny   Yu couldn't speak any English.

Ade   Teacher asked yu to look after me. Yu were my friend. Yu made my life hell.

Kenny   Wat did I do?

Ade   Wat didn't yu do.

Kenny   Yu were holdin me back.

Ade   From all yer white friends.

Kenny   Yu were stupid.

Ade   I was a foreigner. But it's awright Kenny, it's awright. I forgive yu.

Kenny   Why?

Ade   Why not?

Kenny   Yu think yer such a hot guy now, cos yer done yer body up? I ain't impressed. Hangin round wid us like yer a mate or summin. Come on, wat yu want? Tell me.

Ade   Gonna beat me up if I don't?

Kenny   I never touched yu.

Ade   Too busy lettin yer white friends do it. But I understand, why Kenny, yu wanted respect, yu didn't want them pickin on yu.

Kenny   I looked after myself.

Ade   Blatant lie.

Kenny   Oh look, juss fuck off, kunta, yeah.

Ade   I'm gonna forget yu said that. This time. But yu call me that again and I'm gonna hurt yu bad, yu understand me?

Kenny   I ain't afraid of yu.

Ade   Kenny, Kenny, wat made us so different, man? Tell me summin, yu think a white man sees us any different?

Kenny   We are different.

Ade   Wat is it with yu West Indians? Yu bin hangin round wid Ben too long.

Kenny   Move.

Ade   He's fucked yu up. and yu know why, cos yu were too busy kissin up dem white boys' backsides.

Kenny   I've heard this shit before.

Ade   Wantin to be like 'em.

Kenny   There ain't nuttin wrong wid me.

Ade   Why yu think they beat me up? Cos deh were scared of me, of wat I can do.

Kenny   Right.

Ade   I bet yu wanna marry a white girl. Breed wid one a' dem. Thass sad.

Kenny   Wat yu tink I am?

Ade   Kenny, yu juss admitted to me yu got a hard-on. Yer still lettin Ben Harper lead yu round like a dog. Yu gotta tink, brudda. Fuck 'em yeah, by all means, but don't breed wid dem.

Kenny   I do think. I ain't lettin no white guy run tings.

Ade   Oh, so yer runnin tings?

Kenny   Exactly.

Ade   Well I ain't seein much results.

Kenny   I don't care wat yer seein.

Ade   Look at me. Look at me, Kenny. Look at all dem gal. Beautiful, young, white gal. Ready. Ripe. Choose one, choose any gal for me and I got twenty quid in my pocket that says I'll score. Wat yu don't believe? Three white girls are starin at me right now. Left over yer shoulder, girl in blue dancin wid sum bloke. On my right redhead standin by the bar wearing black, chattin wid her mates. Some blonde bit, sitting down drinkin a Coke, to yer left. See wat I mean? Still say yer runnin tings? When's the last time yu fucked a girl, Kenny? Fuck? Pussy?

Kenny   None of yer business.

Ade   Come on, bro to bro.

Kenny   It's none of yer business. I juss have, thass all yu need to know. (**Ade** *starts sniffing him.*) Get off me.

Ade   Yu sure yu had pussy?

Kenny   Yes.

Ade   I ain't smellin no pussy.

Kenny   I have.

Ade   So when yu lass have it?

Kenny   Couple of months ago.

Ade   Name?

Kenny   Debbie.

Ade   Yu lie bad.

Kenny   I'm not lyin.

Ade   Fuck me, man.

Kenny   Yeah, fuck yu.

Ade   Yu gotta be the only one I know.

Kenny   I'm not lyin.

Ade   Does Ben know?

Kenny   Listen.

Ade   And yu a bro too!

Kenny   I'm tellin yer . . .

Ade   Do yu not feel the tiniest bit of shame?

Kenny   Her name was Debbie.

Ade   How old are yu?

Kenny   I met her in a bar.

Ade   Yer sad fucker.

Kenny   It's the truth awright.

Ade   Go stand over deh.

Ben *comes out of the loo and joins his mates.*

Ben   Yu bag some trim yet, Ade?

Ade   Eyeing one up now.

Ben   Who who! (*Looks.*) Wat, that fat one?

Ade   Na thass Kenny's.

Ben   Yer like 'em big, ennit, Kenny? Yu shoulda seen this bird he pulled a couple of years back, Ade, sum real fat bitch. He had his hands all over her flabby legs and flabby arse man. Best he could get. Ennit, Ken, Kenny?

Kenny   Get off me.

Ben   Awright don't cry.

Kenny   Yer the one who's gonna be cryin.

Ben   Look how fat her arse is.

Kenny   Yu hear wat I said?

Ben   Yu could show a film on it.

Kenny   Ben?

Ben   Yeah, bitch, I'm chattin about yu.

Kenny   Did yu hear wat I said, Ben?

Ben   She's tellin her man on me.

Ade   Yu ain't 'fraid?

Ben   Do I look 'fraid?

Kenny   Don't talk to me like that again.

Ben (*to the boyfriend*)   And yer a fat cunt as well, deal wid it.

Kenny (*grabs* **Ben**)   I'll buss yu up right. (**Ben** *laughs*.) Don't laugh at me.

Ben   Yer are so moany.

Ade (*sees someone approaching*)   Awright, take it easy, man, we don't wan no trouble yeah.

Ben   No, let the wanker come, man.

Without warning and out of nowhere, **Kenny** *shoves his mates out of the way and darts over to the dance floor.*

Kenny   Yu wanna a fuckin go, come! (*Runs off.*)

Ben   Kenny! I have never seen him lose it like that! He's gonna get killed.

Ade   Go help him then.

Ben   I ain't goin on my own, yu mad? Nuh, man.

Ade   Don't call me man.

Ben (*confused*)   Ade?

Ade   Yu think yu have the right to speak like us now?

Ben   Come on.

Ade   Is that how it goes now? Yu have the right? Yu stupid white bastard.

Ben   Don't . . .

Ade   Don't call yu that? (*Starts prodding him hard.*) Yu – are – a – stupid – white – bastard! I remember yu. Come on then. (*Shoves him.*) Come on.

Ben (*getting scared*)   Ade, man?

Ade   Yu deaf? Don't call me man.

Ben   We gotta help Kenny.

Ade   Yu help him. (*Exits.*)

Scene Five

Nathan's *front door step. Same evening.*

Kenny *is standing by the door which is ajar.* **Nathan** *appears, he hands* **Kenny** *a glass of water.*

Kenny   Wass this?

Nathan   Water fer yer head. Yu'll thank me in the mornin.

Kenny   Come out for a drink I said.

Nathan We were havin an early night.

Kenny Yu fuckin lightweight.

Nathan Oh Kenny, man, wat yu doin here, wat yu want?

Kenny I missed yer.

Nathan (*embarrassed*) Fuck off.

Kenny It's true.

Nathan Yer pissed.

Kenny I know.

Nathan *hands him some photos.*

Kenny Dis Zoe?

Nathan All eight pounds of her.

Kenny Fuck.

Nathan Thass wat Melanie kept saying, all through the delivery.

Kenny Yu saw it come out?

Nathan Nuttin like it.

Kenny Errgh, man.

Nathan She was holdin on to my hand, nearly broke it off.

Kenny Yu didn't feel sick or nuttin?

Nathan How could I feel sick. It was my kid. So wat yu think of her?

Kenny Yeah, man, she's nice.

Nathan Nice!

Kenny Awright she's beautiful.

Nathan Thass better. Yu can keep that one.

Kenny Nice one, Nate.

Nathan   Tell yer, man, no matter who yu are, how hard yu think yu are, when yu see that little baby for the first time yeah, and yu know it's yours, part of yu, yer gone.

Kenny   Good feeling?

Nathan   The best. I was born for this.

Kenny   She looks like Melanie.

Nathan   It's the cheeks, ennit? Yu don't think she's got my eyes? I think she's got my eyes.

Kenny   The poor cow's got enuff to worry about.

Nathan   Oi!

Kenny   Having yu fer a dad.

Nathan   Gimme back my picture.

Kenny   Move. Yu a dad, man. Shit, Nate!

Nathan   Ennit. I have to keep tellin myself, it don't feel true, hasn't quite sunk in, me a dad.

Kenny   Can't wait to see yu pushing a buggie about. Daddy Nathan.

Nathan   Yu won't be.

Kenny   Come again?

Nathan   We're moving to Manchester.

Kenny   When?

Nathan   As soon as we've found a house we like.

Kenny   We got houses in London, Nate.

Nathan   It's Melanie, she wants to move back closer to her mum.

Kenny   Wat do yu want?

Nathan   I got wat I want.

Kenny   Right little Midas.

Nathan   Wass that mean?

Kenny   Nuttin.

Nathan   Don't do a Ben on me.

Kenny   I ain't.

Nathan   I'm happy awright.

Kenny   Wat did I juss say?

Nathan   Yu are such a prick.

Kenny   Nate?

Nathan   Yu know this could be yu as well one day. I could be looking at pictures of yer kid. Stop getting led around by Ben all the time, yu muppet.

Kenny   He's gettin led round by me.

Nathan   The Palais!

Kenny   I like it deh.

Nathan   That bloke coulda killed yer tonight.

Kenny   He was lucky I didn't kill him. He was. Shoulda seen me, man, gave him a right caning.

Nathan   I'm gonna slap yu so hard in a minute.

Kenny   Rah, Nate turn bad man now.

Nathan   Talk to me.

Kenny   Bwoy, move. Yu love to chat.

Nathan   Wass goin on wid yu?

Kenny   Nuttin.

Nathan   Wat were yu thinking?

Kenny   I said it was nuttin.

Nathan   Don't gimme me that.

Kenny   Look, Ben started shoutin yeah . . .

Nathan   Ben!

Kenny   Let me finish, man.

Nathan   Yu'd jump in the Thames if Ben said.

Kenny   No.

Nathan   Are yu a sheep or wat?

Kenny   I said no.

Nathan   Still going to that dump.

Kenny   Fuck off.

Nathan   Yu fuck off. Yu wonder why I had to leave.

Kenny   I thought it was cos of Ben, know the truth now though. Yu wanted to get away from both of us.

Nathan   Yu were both doing my head in, I needed to go.

Kenny   And ware did yu go, Nate? Half a mile down the road, juss round the corner from me mum's? Twelve months I don't see yu, a whole year, not a phone call, man, nuttin.

Nathan   Yu would never have left Ben, yer too loyal.

Kenny   Is it my fault de bwoy love to hang round wid me?

Nathan   Will yu stop talkin like that. Will yu stop talkin shit. Why do yu love making an arsehole of yourself, every day of your life?

Kenny   Hey, I had enuff of yu dissing me, right.

Nathan   So go. Piss off. But don't bother coming back.

Kenny   I fuckin hate yu.

Nathan   Cos yu know I'm right. Yu pillock.

Kenny   Awright, man, ease up on the abuse.

Nathan   No. Grow up, yu stupid sap, Ben won't.

Ben (*enters*)   Ben won't wat? Kenny bwoy!

Kenny (*surprised*) Ben?

Ben Wat were yu doin runnin off like that?

Kenny Wat are yu?

Ben Lookin for yu. I was worried, man. That bloke gave yu a right beating. Yu awright?

Kenny Yeah

Ben That bloke didn't catch yer? Then again yu were runnin fast enuff.

Kenny I'm fine.

Ben Good. So, Ben won't wat?

Nathan Grow up.

Ben He still loves chattin behind people's back.

Nathan I juss told yu didn't I? I'm going back to bed. (*To* **Kenny**.) Come round for dinner one night.

Ben (*laughs*) Dinner?

Nathan Any time.

Ben Yu can't cook.

Nathan How yu know?

Ben I know.

Nathan So I can't learn?

Ben Must be Melanie. (*Swipes one of the photos.*) Who dis?

Kenny Careful.

Ben Who's the foetus?

Kenny Ben!

Ben She's tiny.

Nathan She is my daughter.

Ben   Melanie finally dropped it then? Wass she doin wid red hair?

Nathan   She ain't got red hair.

Ben (*to* **Kenny**)   I bet the milkman's got red hair.

Nathan   Night, boys.

Ben   Night, Nathan.

Nathan   One of these days, Ben.

Ben   Yeah, wat?

Nathan   One of these fuckin days right.

Ben   Yeah wat!

Kenny   Guys, come on!

Nathan   Three hours on the train, thass all it is.

Ben   Fuckin snide.

Nathan   Wat did I do that was so wrong?

Ben (*teases*)   Ooooh!

Nathan   Juss tell me.

Ben   Kenny, give him a tissue, I think he's gonna cry.

Nathan   Such a wanker.

Ben   Excuse me?

Nathan   Yer not happy unless everyone is as sad as yu.

Ben   Yeah, come back here and say that to my face, Nathan.

Nathan   Talk to the door, Ben. (*Slams door behind him.*)

Ben   Come back and say that to my face. (*To* **Kenny**.) He's a snide right! Wat yu doin here?

Kenny   I jus wanted to see him. Wat were yu?

Ben (*cuts in*)   Three hours on the train, wass that?

Kenny They're movin to Manchester.

Ben Good.

Kenny Yu don't mean that.

Ben I don't care if I never see him again.

Kenny Yer lying.

Ben He's a fuckin snide.

Scene Six

The Palais.

Kenny *is facing* **Sandra***. It is an uncomfortable silence.*

Sandra So yu work in a bank then?

Kenny Yep. Assistant manager.

Sandra Oh yeah! I know who I'm comin to for a loan.

Kenny How long yu known Sonya?

Sandra 'Bout three years. Yu don't look alike.

Kenny Good. Wat yu do?

Sandra Yu've asked me that.

Kenny Sorry.

Sandra Twice.

Kenny Yu keepin score?

Sandra Why yu so jumpy?

Kenny I ain't.

Sandra Like yu 'fraid of me, man. Never seen a black woman before?

Kenny Don't be stupid.

Sandra Ever bin out wid a black woman?

Kenny Yeah.

Sandra Wat about white women?

Kenny Wat yu goin on wid?

Sandra Do yu ever go for white women, Kenny?

Kenny No.

Sandra Not even once?

Kenny No.

Sandra Yer not lyin to me.

Kenny I don't lie.

Sandra Good, cos if yer one of dem fools, dem dogs who hang here chasin white skirt, yu can juss step.

Kenny No worries.

Sandra I don't know why yer sister chose to have her party here yu nuh. The state of these white girls, man, yu see 'em? Wid their high heels, tons of slap on their face.

Kenny Yeah.

Sandra Tell me summin, yer a man right. Right?

Kenny Yeah.

Sandra So wat is it about these fuckin girls that makes our men keep running to them? We got the same bits on our body as them. But the minute one of dem whores walks into a room yeah, all the men are runnin round like dogs, drooling over 'em. It makes me sick. Why do they do that?

Kenny Can't help yer.

Sandra Are white girls more sexy than we are? I don't think so. Do they scream more when guys do it to them? I can scream, I can scream loud.

Kenny I dunno.

Sandra   Come on, Kenny, yu musta heard summin over the years, wat do black guys say, wat do they feel? Why do they do it?

Kenny   I don't know.

Sandra   Wass the matter wid yu?

Kenny   Nuttin. Maybe . . .

Sandra   Wat?

Kenny   Maybe they're scared of yer.

Sandra   Thass a lame excuse, I heard that shit before. Do I look scary to yu, am I scarin yu?

Kenny   No.

Sandra   So why yu look like yu wanna run fer yer life? Do all black women act the bloody same or summim? Yu know wat, fuck this. Fuck this! Don't blame us cos yu lot are fuckin insecure right? Maybe if yu lot treated us right in the first place, wid sum respect. I'm going for a white guy, yu spearchuckers are killin me. Fuckin black men, man, sorry-arsed niggers, yer brains are in yer dicks. A nice, fit, sincere, good-looking white guy yes! Time this gal felt appreciated.

Kenny   See yer then.

Sandra   Hold up, wait. Rum. Goes right to my head. Never let me near it.

Kenny   Don't drink it. We ain't all like him.

Sandra   Who?

Kenny   Yer boyfriend, ennit.

Sandra   Perceptive Kenneth. I like that. So wass yer story?

Kenny   Ain't got one. Oh don't do that. Why yu lot love to pull that face?

Sandra   Yu lot?

Kenny   Wid the attitude.

Sandra   Yu mean black women?

Kenny   I didn't say black. I meant women. All women.

Sandra   Maybe it's yu.

Kenny   It's yu women as well. Yu know how small yu make me feel? Like that.

Sandra   Don't be so soft. Yu ain't so bad. Yu can't like someone if yu don't like yerself.

Kenny   Wat yu tink yer smart now?

Sandra   Didn't get three A levels for nuttin.

Kenny   Yu get three A levels?

Sandra   Yes, Kenneth. Hear wat, I can read and write an all.

Kenny   So wat yu doin working in Argos wid yer three A levels?

Sandra   It's a job.

Kenny   Yu don't think yer wastin yerself?

Sandra   Yer sister works there.

Kenny   I rest my case.

Sandra   Yu got a nice smile.

Kenny laughs.

Sandra   Why yu so embarrassed by that?

Kenny   Do I look embarrassed?

Sandra   Yes. And I'm gonna bus yer head if yu keep doing that. Ain't no one told yu before got a nice smile? Cos yu have. To die for. Take the compliment.

Kenny   Awright I will.

Sandra   Startin now.

Kenny Right now.

Sandra (*smiles*) Good.

Kenny Yu want go upstairs?

Sandra Why?

Kenny There's another dance floor, it plays better music.

Sandra Thought yu didn't come here.

Kenny I don't. I had a look when I came in.

Sandra And then wat?

Kenny Dance.

Sandra We could dance down here.

Kenny We could go somewhere else.

Sandra And yu were doing so well.

Kenny Look, yes or no, Sandra, yu dont have to run me down.

Sandra Oh Kenny! Don't do a moody on me please. Ain't me thass coming out wid the dry chat. Do I look like I wanna be picked up? I didn't come here for that. I would never come here for that. All I wanna do is chat. If that ain't good enough for yu, then score wid one 'a dem white girls, there's plenty, go.

Kenny It is. It is good enough for me.

Sandra Yu sure?

Kenny I'm sure.

Sandra Yu positive?

Kenny Yeah.

Sandra Don't say yu are if yer not, Kenny.

Kenny I am sure. Love to go on, ennit?

Sandra Yeah. Now get me another drink.

Act Two

Scene One

A street.

Ben *is on his phone.*

Kenny   Hang up. I ain't messin about, hang up.

Ben   It's ringin.

Kenny   I ain't doin it.

Ben   Hello?

Kenny   I ain't doin it.

Ben   Is that (*Reads from the card.*) Cindy? Yeah I saw yer card, I was wondering where yu are. Full personal service, one hour. Is this a genuine photo? Yeah? Yeah! Awright yeah, can I have yer address? Wat? Why yu askin me that? Yu fuckin bitch. Yeah I hope yu get AIDS, yer slag. (*Hangs up suddenly.*)

Kenny   Wat?

Ben   Fuckin whore, man.

Kenny   Wat she say?

Ben   Don't worry about it.

Kenny   Tell me.

Ben   Don't get upset, Kenny, but she wanted to know if I was black. She says she don't do it wid black men. Don't worry about it, man, I still love yer.

Kenny   Who's worried? Yu think I care wat a whore thinks, it don't matter.

Ben   She must have a boyfriend who's black. He don't want another bro touchin her, ennit. She ain't worth the time, Kenny, she's a bitch.

Kenny Can we go home please?

Ben Hold up, let's not give up on the first go. (*Takes out some cards from his wallet.*) There must be one yu like.

Kenny Jesus Christ, how many cards yu got?

Ben Oh man, look at that one.

Kenny Yu really think I wanna do this?

Ben Yer sack is bursting, Kenny. I know how it feels.

Kenny Yu done this before.

Ben Couple of times.

Kenny Why?

Ben I get itches, man.

Kenny Yer married.

Ben Still get 'em. I don't fuck 'em, I juss get a blowjob an that. (*Eyes one.*) Lulu, French. Yeah man! (*Dials.*)

Kenny Ben?

Ben Back off. Yeah, French Beauty Lulu, yeah I see yer card, listen is that a genuine photo, she really looks like that?

Kenny (*grabs the phone*) No.

Ben Come on, she ain't no dog.

Kenny No. (*Hangs up.*)

Ben I'll go after yu.

Kenny For fuck's sake!

Ben Yu know wat, this is the lass time I ever do yu a favour.

Kenny Yu call this a favour?

Ben Juss get yer cock sucked.

Kenny And yu wonder why Nate don't wanna see us.

Ben   Nathan's a cunt. Marries sum bit, thinks he knows it all. Come on Kenny man, it's help me, help yu time. Look at her picture, look at her tits, don't tell me yu don't want 'em in yer face.

Kenny   I don't.

Ben   All I want to do is help yu catch up with Ade. He's had nuff pussy.

Kenny   Hear wat, so have I.

Ben   Wat, yu found yerself a woman now?

Kenny   Yes.

Ben   Lie.

Kenny   I have.

Ben   Yu ain't, Kenny.

Kenny   Is that so strange?

Ben   Name?

Kenny   Sandra.

Ben   Sandra? Is that the best yu can do?

Kenny   It's her bloody name, awright?

Ben   Come on.

Kenny   I ain't making it up, Ben.

Ben   Serious?

Kenny   Yes.

Ben   Well gimme sum details then. Ware yu meet her, who is she, how long?

Kenny   She's a mate of my sister's, we met at the Palais a couple of nights ago.

Ben   Nice one, bro. I bet she's white though, ennit, slapper!

Kenny   She's black.

Ben   Yu joke! (*Roars.*) Kenny boy, doing it wid him own kind at last. All the more reason to see this whore. Black women go like a train yeah? Yu don't get match fit, she'll run yu ragged.

Kenny   I'm going home.

Ben   Yer gettin yer cock sucked. And a fuck while yer at it.

Kenny   I don't need to.

Ben   Yu tellin me yu fucked it awready?

Kenny   Yeah, I fucked it awready. She can't get enough of it. I got it, Ben. Hard to believe I know, but I finally got someone an it's real.

Ben   Yu'll screw it up. Yu always do.

Kenny   Watch yer mouth.

Ben   Or wat! Wat do yu think yu can do to me, Kenneth? Wat did yu think yu could ever do to me? Yu think yer black, yu tink yer bad? Yu get a few pokes and yu tink yu the man? Yu want wake up. I know yu! I bet yu can't even do it properly. Juss behave yerself and do wat yer told right, or do yu want that girl laughin at yu every time yer givin her one?

Kenny   I'm goin home.

Ben (*waves the card*)   Yu want it?

Kenny   Denise is waiting for yer.

Ben   38DD. (*Dials.*)

Kenny   Why did yu go to Nathan's that time?

Ben   I was lookin for yu.

Kenny   But yu hate his guts. Why did yu go?

Ben   Still engaged.

Kenny   Yu wanted to see him, cos yu were missin him, ennit? Cos this ain't yu, it ain't neither of us, why can't yu admit that? Go home, Ben.

Ben   I don't wanna go home. I don't want to see her face ever again.

Kenny   So she's got big teeth.

Ben   I didn't even fancy her. Yu know wat I did this morning, when I woke up? Started yawning and stretching right, 'member wat I said? Whacked her right in the face wid my elbow. Not one of her teeth come out. Not one! She still looks the same, Kenny. Wat they made of, iron?

Kenny   Yu hit yer wife.

Ben   I made out it was an accident, but she wouldn't stop cryin.

Kenny   Wass the matter wid yu? She's your wife. She is all yer ever gonna get.

Ben   I'll get loads, Kenny, I've had loads.

Kenny   Yu've had whores.

Ben   Go. Go and be laughed at by yer black woman. Amount of pussy I coulda had in my life, but nuh, had to hang round wid yu and only cos the black kids couldn't stand yu. Yu were a joke to them. Yu were lucky me and Nate took pity on yer, everyone was tellin us to drop yer.

Kenny   So drop me now. Do it. (**Kenny** *walks away*.)

Ben   She's laughin at yu, Ken, she's pissin herself.

Ben *presses his redial button again.*

Ben   Hello? Lulu ? Yeah I saw yer card. How much for an hour? Where are yer?

Scene Two

Palais nightclub.

Ade *is with* **Sandra**.

Ade   . . . So wass this guy's name?

Sandra   None of yer business.

Ade   I might know him.

Sandra   Yu don't.

Ade   How yu know?

Sandra   Go away.

Ade   Whoever he is, he muss be really special, if yer out in that dress. Yu aways look good in this dress. (*Squeezes her thigh.*)

Sandra   Get yer hand off me.

Ade   Easy, gal.

Sandra   I ain't yer gal.

Ade   Wat yu doin here, Sandra?

Sandra   Havin a drink.

Ade   Yu wouldn't be seen dead comin here. It's cos of me, ennit?

Sandra   Yu wish.

Ade   So wass this guy like?

Sandra   Yer white slag's wavin to yer.

Ade   'Im givin it to yu good?

Sandra   Dirty bastard.

Ade   Does he stroke the back of yer neck like I used to?

Sandra   He's juss a friend.

Ade   Friend!

Sandra   Go away, please.

Ade   Nuh, man, I'm stayin right here till 'yer friend' comes back.

Sandra   Yu know wat, it muss be sad bin yu, Ade. Havin to prove to yerself, every night, that yer fit, yer all man. Yer come a long way from the shy guy who didn't know ware to put it.

Ade   Hey, I aways knew ware to put it.

Sandra   And when yu finally did, it kept on comin out, 'member? 'Is it in Sandra? Sandra is it in?'

Ade   Yer chattin shit. Bitch.

Sandra   Don't feel too bad, yu were awright, after a while. I bet thass why yu go fer yer white girls, ennit, cos they tink yer givin them the fuck of the century wid yer third leg. See yer one over there, I bet yu only have to touch her and she's creamin her knickers, ennit? But I know the trut, so do a lot of sistas who know niggers like yu.

Ade   Yer frigid.

Sandra   Old.

Ade   Can't handle wass on offer.

Sandra   I've seen bigger ones than yours. Big!

Ade   And yu girls have the nerve to wonder why we go lookin elsewhere.

Sandra   Cos yer sad?

Ade   All yu lot come wid is this attitude, 'is who yu look pon', all that shit. Especially yu, yu love to put that on, yu call that sexy? Every time yu and that bitch Yvonne get together.

Sandra   Don't call my friend a bitch.

Ade Yu know it ain't yu.

Sandra Yer the bitch.

Ade When we first went out, yu had summim.

Sandra Mug, written on my forehead.

Ade Yer mates had nuttin but big mouths on them, but yu were different from them, I saw it the minute I laid eyes on yer.

Sandra Juss hurry up and come fer the rest of yer things right.

Ade Yer better than them and yu know it.

Sandra I am one a' dem! Go back to yer white whore.

Ade So yu find yerself another African prince then. Wat makes yu think he's gonna be any different than me?

Sandra He ain't African.

Ade Yes he is.

Sandra No he ain't.

Ade Don't lie, Sandra.

Sandra I ain't lyin.

Ade I know yu, yu can't help yerself. Yu love yer darkie men too much. I know. Juss like I know that white bitch over there wants me to fuck her tonight.

Sandra Do yu want to go to jail?

Ade Yu jealous?

Sandra Look at her. She don't look much older than yer sister, man. Stay or go, cos I don't care.

Ade Yu do.

Ade *touches her thigh again.* **Sandra** *doesn't push him away until* **Kenny** *enters, carrying drinks.*

Sandra   Kenny. Ware yu bin?

Kenny   Bloody queue was a mile long. Awright, Ade? (*Sits next to* **Sandra**.)

Ade   Him? Yu tellin me it's him?

Sandra   Yu know each other?

Ade   No, no, no, man.

Sandra   No wat?

Ade   I'm not havin it.

Sandra   Yer not havin it?

Ade   Yu and him.

Sandra   It's none of yer business.

Ade   Fuck's sake, gal, him? He ain't nuttin.

Sandra   He ain't yu.

Ade   Awright, Sandra, enuff's enuff yeah wat yu want?

Sandra   I want yu to go.

Ade   Me dump the bitch, fine she's dumped. (*Waves.*) Laters. I don't care about her.

Sandra   Nor do I, fuck whoever yu like.

Ade   But thass all she is, juss a fuck. I don't care about her. I don't care about none of them. Ain't it yu I aways come back to though?

Sandra   Well I'm tired of it yeah. Sick an tired. The way yu make me feel, about myself.

Ade   Well he ain't no better. I fuck 'em cos I can, Sandra. He can't even do that. He's desperate. No white gal will touch him. Look at him, look at him juss fuckin standin there like sum fool.

Sandra   Leave him alone.

Ade   Yu comin?

Sandra   Leave me alone.

Kenny   Come on, Ade.

Ade   YU SHUT YER MOUT! DON'T TOUCH ME!

Sandra   Ade!

Ade   I'm better than yu.

Sandra   Juss go.

Ade   I'm better than yu.

Sandra   Now.

Ade *leaves.*

Sandra   Wass that about?

Kenny   We were at school together

Sandra   And?

Kenny   And nuttin, guy's mad.

Sandra   Wat did he mean white girls wouldn't touch yu? Yer one of dem. I shoulda guessed. Yu come here all the time, ennit?

Kenny   No.

Sandra   Kenny, don't lie.

Kenny   Awright yeah, but I don't do that no more, I swear.

Sandra   Look it's OK. It's none of my business.

Kenny   Yu wanted to come here again, I didn't.

Sandra   If thass wat yu want, gwan. Don't let me stop yer.

Kenny   It's not wat I want. I lied cos I wanted to see yu again.

Sandra   Kenny?

Kenny   I know, yu've told me, yu juss want us to be friends, yu ain't ready for nuttin else.

Kenny *watches* **Sandra** *who in turn is watching* **Ade**.

Kenny   Well I know why yu wanted to come here again.

Sandra   Wat yu take me for?

Kenny   Who's lyin now? Wat did yu see in him?

Sandra   Same thing she does.

Kenny   She ain't all that. Yer fitter than that.

Sandra   Trying to make me feel better, Kenneth?

Kenny   Yeah.

Sandra *leans forward and kisses him on the cheek.* **Kenny** *takes this as read and kisses her back.*

Kenny   Was that awright?

Sandra *laughs.*

Kenny   Wat yu laughin for?

Sandra   It was nice. Yu shouldn't say things like that. Don't look so worried.

Kenny   It's awright, I'm cool.

Sandra   Good.

Kenny   Look when I asked yu was it awright, I didn't mean that I was, that I was, yu know soft cos I ain't right, I ain't like, I juss thought yu wanted me to kiss yu, but I'm sorry if yu didn't.

Sandra   Kenny.

Kenny   SHIT!

Sandra   Will yu please calm down. It's awright. Wat am I going to do wid yu huh?

Sandra *glances over at* **Ade** *again, getting off with his girl. She kisses* **Kenny** *on the lips.*

Sandra   Finish yer drink.

Kenny   Why were we?

Sandra   Come on.

Scene Three

Nathan's *front door step.*

Nathan *opens a Mothercare shopping bag and looks inside.*

Nathan   How much was all this?

Kenny   Don't worry about it, there was a sale.

Nathan   I'm juss trying to picture it. Yu in Mothercare. We got baby clothes coming out of our ears.

Kenny   Now yu got sum more. Yu gonna invite me in or wat?

Nathan   Yeah in a minute, juss let me have this. Melanie don't like me smoking in the house wat wid the baby and that.

Kenny   She's really beautiful.

Nathan   I know. And yer final answer is?

Kenny   I dunno.

Nathan   The christening's in two weeks.

Kenny   Wat yu want a godfather for? Yu don't even go to church.

Nathan   Melanie's mum. She's into all that. I juss do wat I'm told, mate.

Nathan   Makes for a quiet life. Well?

Kenny   I dunno.

Nathan   Wass there to know?

Kenny   It'll feel funny, wat wid Ben.

Nathan   We have to chat about him?

Kenny   Well I don't need to ask ware yu stand on it.

Nathan   Ennit.

Kenny   If he was here now, yu'd be askin him.

Nathan   No.

Kenny   He's still yer best mate.

Nathan   Yes or no, Kenny?

Kenny   I'll think about it.

Nathan   Don't strain yerself.

Kenny   I'm really worried about him. He's never done anything like this before.

Nathan   Why? He brought it on himself.

Kenny   We talkin about the same Ben here?

Nathan   The same Ben who wouldn't come to my wedding, the same Ben who blew me out on his.

Kenny   He ain't no wife beater.

Nathan   He hit her.

Kenny   Well we can't all be like yu. Wid yer nice house, wife, kid.

Nathan   This is Ben talking. I can hear his voice.

Kenny   Yu know he only married her to get back at yu.

Nathan   Wass there to get back at? I fell in love for fuck's sake. This is all so stupid. Can we change the subject please, if yer not going to be Zoe's godfather, least yu can do is stay for dinner? Give Sandra a bell. I want to meet her.

Kenny   She's busy.

Nathan   Wid wat?

Kenny   Work.

Nathan   We'll have to make it next week then. I'll tell Mel. How about Thursday?

Kenny   Watever.

Nathan   Don't sound too eager.

Kenny   Will yu shut up about dinner please, yu sound like a nob.

Nathan   Touchy.

Kenny   Yu love to go on.

Nathan   Awright.

Kenny   Asking me to be godfather. Cos I got a girlfriend now, I'm respectable now.

Nathan   Up to yu.

Kenny   Then wat? We go out on double dates, meal, cinema, be best man at my wedding. We have homes in the country, women at our side, kids at our feet.

Nathan   Don't be a prick all yer life.

Kenny   Couldn't yu have juss fucked Melanie?

Nathan   Say wat yu feel, Ken.

Kenny   Yu shoulda juss fucked her.

Nathan   Yeah I shoulda juss fucked her, like a fucking lad I shoulda fucked her. But there is juss one problem, Kenny, I'm not a lad. I never was. Yeah I had a laugh, I got pissed, but all I was doing was waiting, waiting for someone special to come into my life. Yu got someone special in yer life now, right? Haven't yer?

Kenny   How do I keep her happy, Nate ? How do I do it?

Nathan   Be yerself.

Kenny   Yu always say that, yer always tellin me that, be yerself!

Nathan   And yu never listen.

Kenny   I don't know wat we have.

Nathan   She's yer girlfriend, yu fool.

Kenny   She ain't my girlfriend. We met a couple of weeks ago at my sister's party. We went out lass night, she took me back to hers. Yu know wat I'm saying, yu know were I'm going wid this?

Nathan   Yeah I think so.

Kenny   It was crap. I was crap. I didn't know wat I was doing, not a clue. She knew it too. So nice about it though, made it easy for me, she's always doin that. If thass been myself.

Nathan   Did it ever occur to yu in that stupid head of yours, yu weren't bin yerself, yu spent half yer life thinking about it, how yer gonna do it, but when it comes down to it, yu ain't got a clue.

Kenny   I'm twenty-nine, I should be fuckin her brains out, make her scream her head off.

Nathan   Listen, when I first saw Melanie man, I tell yer, I knew she was the one for me. But that didn't stop me making a prat of myself in front of her. Yu think I knew what we were doing when we first did it? I was well nervous, shaking like fuck. She had to calm me down. But afterwards it didn't matter, cos we were so right for each other.

Kenny   Oh enuff wid that corny shit, Nate.

Nathan   It's true. Laugh all yu want, Kenny, but it's true. For me anyway.

Kenny   But yu said yu were waiting for someone. So yu didn't care who it was. Yu were desperate to be loved. So how different are yu from Ben?

Nathan   I love my wife.

Kenny   Yu only went with her cos she got pregnant, Ben said.

Nathan   Ben's a liar.

Kenny   Yu only knew her five minutes.

Nathan   So wat, who cares how long yu knew her, who cares about anything at all when yer sure about yer feelins? I love Melanie. She's everything to me. I think about her all the time, I hate it when we're apart, we cuddle up to each other in bed all mornin, every Sunday, read the papers. All that corny shit, Kenny, and I love it.

Kenny   Yer the lucky one then.

Nathan   It can still happen to yu.

Kenny   So wat I can't come in now?

Nathan   Up to yu.

Kenny   She's me god-daughter.

Scene Four

Sandra's *flat.*

Sandra *watches as* **Ade** *comes into the living room carrying his bag.*

Ade   Right, got the rest of my things, I'm gone yeah.

Sandra   So which one of dem slags yu movin in wid then?

Ade   I thought yu didn't wanna talk to me?

Sandra   I don't.

Ade   So why yu chattin?

Sandra   I need an address. To forward yer mail.

Ade   Yu couldn't juss ask me that?

Sandra   Don't read anything into that.

Ade   Am I?

Sandra   I know yer looks.

Ade   I'm still at me mum's. Awright?

Sandra   Thank yu. Goodbye.

Ade (*takes a video from his bag*)   Sure yu don't want this one?

Sandra   Why?

Ade   It's good.

Sandra   It's French.

Ade   Yes or no?

Sandra   No. Yu better not have messed up my Buffy collection.

Ade   Heaven forbid. I suppose yu'll be movin him in now.

Sandra   No.

Ade   Yu love him?

Sandra   I told yu.

Ade   He's juss a friend, yeah watever. Can't believe I let this happen, yu nuh.

Sandra   Yu let this happen?

Ade   Runnin to him.

Sandra   Lass time I checked, Ade, I had a mind of my own.

Ade (*takes out another video*)   Wat about this?

Sandra   No.

Ade   It won four Oscars.

Sandra   I don't want yer videos. I don't want nuttin of yours in my flat.

Ade   Did he tell yu what him and his mates did to me at school?

Sandra   Yeah.

Ade   And?

Sandra   Ain't my fault yu couldn't stick up for yerself.

Ade   Yu sound like the teachers.

Sandra   Was it that bad?

Ade   Yeah it was.

Sandra   Don't take it out on me.

Ade   Wat do yu expect when I find yer goin wid him, why him, Sandra!

Sandra   I'm talking about the past two years.

Ade   Twice, I fucked around twice.

Sandra   Three times, don't lie. And those are the ones I know about.

Ade   Well blame him then.

Sandra   Yu ain't got a mind of yer own?

Ade   Every mornin when I had to go into that school, I was shakin wid fear. Till I was fifteen. Every single day his precious white friends takin turns beating me up. I didn't know who I hated more, him or dem.

Sandra   So yu wanna hurt them now?

Ade   Yeah.

Sandra   And yu wanna fuck deh women, no matter who yu hurt along the way.

Ade   I didn't mean to.

Sandra   But yu did. Yu don't do that. Yu don't take me wid yu. Wat I am, wat we had, should be enough for yu.

Ade   I'm sorry.

Sandra   Fuck sorry. I had it wid sorry. Yu know wat, I don't think yu hate 'em cos they beat yu up. I think yu hate 'em cos they chose Kenny and not yu.

Ade   Wat?

Sandra   All dem white boys. Kenny standin wid dem.

Ade   Were yu there?

Sandra   Yu wanted to be standin wid dem.

Ade   Yu weren't bloody there.

Sandra   Tell me I'm wrong.

Ade   Laters.

Sandra   Ade?

Ade   Fuck off.

Sandra   Look me in the eye.

Ade   Yer talkin shit.

Sandra   Look me in the eye. Tell me yu weren't lyin on the ground yeah, getting kicked around, thinking to yerself, 'Choose me, choose me, I'm better than he is, choose me!'

Ade   No.

Sandra   True, ennit?

Ade   No.

Sandra   Ade? It's true.

Ade   Fuck off.

Sandra   Knew it.

Ade   Yu don't know nuttin.

Sandra   I know. Yu were juss too dark.

Ade   Yu fuckin cow. Yu think I wanna be white?

Sandra   Don't yu? Tell the truth, Ade. Juss once tell me the truth please.

Ade   No.

Sandra   Yer lying.

Ade   I don't want to be white.

Sandra   Yes yu do.

Ade   Sandra!

Sandra   And yu want the same for me. Ennit? Ennit? Ain't that the answer, Ade?

Ade   The answer's no.

Sandra   So why yu always telling me I'm better than my friend?

Ade   Cos yu are.

Sandra   Confusing the fuck outta me. The worst thing is, I know yer right. I spoke to Yvonne, New Year's Eve?

Ade   She tell yu?

Sandra   It's wat she didn't say. Look on her face when I brought it up. Tek that fuckin smile off yer face.

Ade   I weren't smilin.

Sandra   I feel it every day, is that wat yu wanna hear? Hearin her and them go on about shit, runnin men down, mek up noise wherever they are. I feel like killin them sometimes. When I'm wid dem, people don't see me, they see black.

Ade   Feisty nigger woman wid attitude.

Sandra   I don't like it when I think like that. And I ain't ready to step out, Ade, especially to be with you. Yu want everything from me but yu give back nuttin.

Ade   Yu think yer gonna get that from him?

Kenny   He will suck the life out of yu. I ain't gonna stand round and let that happen.

Sandra   Yu don't have a say in wat happens to me.

Ade   Yu can't tell me all that about yer friends and expect me to walk. Not when there's a chance.

Sandra   Why are yu doin this to me?

Ade   I don't want yu seein him.

Sandra   Why yu love doing this to me?

Ade   Yu know he can't make yu feel better than I can.

Sandra   Yer as screwed up as he is.

Ade   Don't compare me to him.

Sandra   Why not? Why can't I do that, wat yu afraid of?

Ade   I'm done with white women.

Sandra   I don't want to hear yu, I don't want to see yu.

Ade   I don't need them.

Sandra   Do I look like I care?

Ade   I got yu, all I wanted was yu, the real yu. We stay in and watch telly all day like we used to yeah? When we first went out. I go out for KFC. Then we stay in bed all evening and watch *Blind Date*. Sandra?

Sandra   No.

Ade   Come on.

Sandra   I ain't letting yu confuse me.

Ade   I'm not.

Sandra   Yu are, Ade. Yu bloody are.

Scene Five

Sandra*'s flat.* **Kenny** *is typing away on his laptop.*

Kenny   How much do yu think yu can save each month?

Sandra   Dunno. Forty?

Kenny   That all?

Sandra   Wat?

Kenny   Yu won't see much of a pension wid that?

Sandra   It's all I can afford.

Kenny   How much yu earn a week?

Sandra   A hundred and ninety.

Kenny   That all?

Sandra   Yes!

Kenny   Ain't much.

Sandra   It'll do me.

Kenny   Yu got this place.

Sandra   Housing Association.

Kenny   But it's nice.

Sandra   Oi! Do yu know how much rent I'd be paying if sum landlord had his hands on it? Yu know ware I'd be? Back at me mum's.

Kenny   Yu should speak to someone from yer own bank. Ask to speak to yer financial consultant.

Sandra   All I want is advice.

Kenny   Not my special field though.

Sandra   Yer a bloody bank manager.

Kenny   Assistant. Awright, yu want to see a decent pension, start putting a few coins in.

Sandra   So how much then?

Kenny   'Bout a hundred? Hey, don't knock it, keep saving, and yu could have a hundred thousand by the time yer sixty. Juss buy a few less CDs a month.

Sandra   Shut up.

Kenny   Or video.

Kenny *kisses* **Sandra**. **Sandra** *pretends to enjoy it.*

Sandra   More wine? (*Goes in the kitchen.*) Look, I don't know if I can afford a hundred.

Kenny   Yu can, see yer . . .

Sandra   Financial consultant, I heard.

Kenny   Have I done summin?

Sandra   Wat?

Kenny   Yer in a mood.

Sandra   And it has to be about yu.

Kenny   Sorry.

Sandra   Stop apologising. Bad day at work.

Kenny   Wanna talk?

Sandra   No. Put that away.

Kenny   Yu wanted my advice.

Sandra   Yu've advised.

Kenny   Look why don't we get married!

Sandra (*stunned*)   Excuse me?

Kenny   Married.

Sandra   Oh man.

Kenny   Yer the one.

Sandra   Kenny?

Kenny   Don't we?

Sandra   We need to talk.

Kenny   No, don't say that.

Sandra   Yu expect me to say yes right now?

Kenny   Yu think I bin sudden.

Sandra   Wat yu on, man?

Kenny   Well so wat? Who cares about bin sudden, who cares about anythin when yer sure about yer feelins? I am. At least think about it yeah, don't come out wid we gotta talk.

Sandra   Yu don't love me, Kenny, yu juss love the idea.

Kenny   Yu fucked him.

Sandra   I'm sorry?

Kenny   All his videos have gone.

Sandra   He came round today to get his stuff.

Kenny   Then yu fucked him and yer going back to him.

Sandra   Kenny . . .

Kenny   Guys like him, man, all my life.

Sandra   Listen to me.

Kenny   Don't yu think I wanna be like him, like all of them?

Sandra   I did not fuck him. I wanted to. I thought about it. But I didn't do it.

Kenny   Oh man. Come here. Come here.

Sandra   Kenny.

Kenny (*kisses her*)   I really thought that was it yu nuh, total blow out, game over, same old shit.

Sandra   Kenny wait, juss wait man. I ain't gonna marry yu.

Kenny   But the other night though.

Sandra   Wass sex. Fer fuck's sake.

Kenny   Awright, we'll carry on as before then.

Sandra   No.

Kenny   Why?

Sandra   Yu know why. Jeez, yu men are doing my head in. I can't carry yu.

Kenny   That wat it feels like?

Sandra   Yes.

Kenny   It never happens, it never happens to me. I'm aways missin out, me. Yu know why, cos, cos, I can't get a handle on it yu know. Never know wat to do. I see a girl right, look at her and that, she looks back, yer heart's goin mad, tellin yu thass it, go fer it, but yer head, fuckin head right, fuckin head sayin na, na, don't be silly, yer wrong, man! So yu give it up, yer let it go. But wat if it was right, that was it, she was the one, wat if I juss said summin, stop believin that yer crap, yer nuttin, and believed, juss believed she liked yer. I don't have to think, I don't have to do nuttin, or prove myself, fuck wat colour yu are, fuck how yu think yu look, juss feel it, let yerself feel it.

Kenny *packs away his laptop. He takes* **Sandra***'s hand and kisses it before leaving.*

Scene Six

Palais Nightclub.

Ben *is with* **Kenny**.

Kenny   I wasn't sweatin. My heart weren't pumpin. Or shakin like a leaf. None of that. Not a trace of wat went on before. Nerves of steel. I juss did it.

Ben Was she white?

Kenny Yes.

Ben Whore. Find yerself a black woman, wass the matter wid yer?

Kenny I did remember.

Ben Stealin our women!

Kenny Kiss my shiny black arse awright.

Ben So yu asked this whore out then?

Kenny Yes.

Ben So wat she say?

Kenny She went all embarrassed, face was turnin red, man, I was thinkin, oh fuck, blow out, feel like a right turd.

Ben Nuttin unusual about that.

Kenny I was thinkin again, when am I ever gonna get it right?

Ben She said no.

Kenny No.

Ben She said yes?!

Kenny Yes.

Ben She said yes to yu?

Kenny Yes.

Ben Gwan.

Kenny Thank yu.

Ben Gwan!

Kenny She gave me her number.

Ben Yu call her?

Kenny Yeah.

Ben   Details!

Kenny   I called her.

Ben   And?

Kenny   Left a message on her machine.

Ben   She called yu back, and?

Kenny   She didn't.

Ben   Wat?

Kenny   Called me back.

Ben   Wat yu mean she didn't call yu back?

Kenny   She didn't call me back.

Ben   Yu asked for her number, she gave it yer.

Kenny   No, I didn't ask for her number, she juss gave it to me.

Ben   So why ain't she called yu back?

Kenny   Ask her.

Ben   Fuckin whore.

Kenny   Rang her back twice.

Ben   Wass she say?

Kenny   Nuttin, spoke to the machine.

Ben   Fuckin whore.

Kenny   Oh well.

Ben   Wat yu mean 'oh well'? This is bad, man.

Kenny   I know it is.

Ben   So wat yu smilin for?

Kenny   Yu want me go goin back bin miserable? I weren't nervous. I saw her, liked her, asked her out. Thinkin didn't come into it. I juss did it.

Ben   She blew yu out, yu fool.

Kenny   Her loss.

Ben   Denzil!

Kenny   I ain't bodered no more.

Ben   Wat brought this on?

Kenny   Nuttin.

Ben   It was that Sandra slag.

Kenny   Don't call her that.

Ben   Slag, man.

Kenny   Ben! Wat the fuck.

Ben   Wass that mean?

Kenny   It means wat it means, wat the fuck.

Ben   Juss hurry up and find a woman, man.

Kenny   Yes, Dad.

Ben   A black woman, leave our ones alone.

Kenny   I heard yu rang Nathan.

Ben   Yeah, I thought I might as well, yu know. He's suffered enough.

Kenny   Wat did yu say?

Ben   Don't be a stranger, keep in touch.

Kenny   Nice one.

Ben   He really loves her, ennit?

Kenny   Yeah.

Ben   Denise's kicked me out.

Kenny   Yeah?

Ben   Her dad wants me dead.

Kenny   Wat about yer job?

Ben   Fuck yer job. His words.

Kenny (*sees his friend crying*)   Ben?

Ben (*wipes his face*)   Juss find yerself a nice girl, Kenny, awright.

Kenny   Awright.

Ben   Yu deserve one.

Kenny   Thanks.

Blackout.

Sing Yer Heart Out for the Lads

Act One

*King George Public House, south-west London. This section of the bar area is decorated with flags of St George. Windows, walls tables, etc. A huge TV screen is draped in the corner. **Jimmy** is assembling rows of stools and chairs in front of the TV screen. **Gina**, his daughter, is writing names on stickers with a felt-tip pen and sellotaping them on the stools, one by one.*

Gina There had better not be any trouble.

Jimmy Lee will be here.

Gina Lee?

Jimmy He'll sort 'em out.

Gina Lee is juss as bad as they are.

Jimmy He's a copper.

Gina Yer point being?

Jimmy He's a copper, Gina, nuff said.

Gina Get a few pints down him, you'll see. I should know.

She looks at her dad who has the remote for the telly.

You awright over there, Dad?

Jimmy Can't get this fuckin thing to work.

Gina Well, I don't want to hear that, do I?

Jimmy (*looks at screen*) Fucking static.

Gina Leave it to me. (*Takes the remote.*) Wat you done?

Jimmy Nuttin, I was . . .

Gina Pissin about.

Jimmy Oi!

Gina *presses the button on the remote. The screen becomes all blue.*

Jimmy   Piece of shit.

Gina   You finish with the names, I'll do this.

Jimmy   You put Lawrie at the front?

Gina   Yeah. On second thoughts, stick him near the back. He'll only piss about. (*To TV.*) Come on, come on!

Jimmy   Ain't workin.

Gina   The satellite signal ain't comin through. Dad, do me a favour, check that the cable for the dish is plugged in.

Jimmy   Have already.

Gina   What about the dish outside?

Jimmy   Done that.

Gina   Then what is its fucking problem? Where's the instruction manual?

Jimmy   Behind the bar.

Gina   Well, giss it. (**Jimmy** *hands over the manual.*) If I said it once, I've said it a hundred times.

Jimmy   Oh don't start.

Gina   Becks is nuttin but a thievin little git. You should know better.

Jimmy   It was a steal.

Gina   Here we go. Come on, baby, come on, come on . . . (*A picture comes on.*) Yes!

Jimmy   It'll be typical if they called the match off. It's pissing down. We ain't gonna win.

Gina   That's patriotic.

Jimmy   Kevin Keegan is a fucking muppet. Have you seen his line-up? (*Holds up paper.*) Tosser!

Gina   A bit of faith, Dad.

Jimmy   Bollocks. He oughta fuck off back to Fulham, be Al Fayed's bleeding lapdog! Never mind manage the national team. A bit of faith, my arse!

Gina   What's wrong?

Jimmy   Southgate. Keegan has given him the midfield holding position. The midfield holding position, I have trouble even saying it. Look, Southgate is a defender, bloody good one, no argument, but a good passer of the ball, he ain't! I mean Keegan's got Dennis Wise in the frame, why didn't he pick him? Use him? If that ain't torture for the lad, to be picked for the squad, but only to be left on the touchline, whilst some muppet makes a right bollock of the position he's blinding at. I ask you, where's the sense?

Gina   Southgate might surprise everyone.

Jimmy   Yeah, he'll be more shittier than I thought.

Gina   You won't be watchin the match then. You can clear out the backyard at last.

Jimmy   Now, I didn't say I weren't gonna watch it. I'm juss stating my opinion, thass all.

Gina   Who's up front?

Jimmy   Owen and Cole. Andy fucking Cole. Our last game at Wembley an'all. Fucking Keegan.

Gina   Does Andy Gray's face look blue to you?

Jimmy   Very.

Gina   I can't work out anything on this.

Jimmy   Let one of the boys do it. Look at his poxy formation.

Gina   Dad!

Jimmy   3–5–2! Poxy, continental shit!

Gina   Let me guess, 4–4–2?

Jimmy   Too right, 4–4–2. It's the English way of playing: go with summin the lads are comfortable with, fer crying out loud. 3–5–2!

Gina   Dad, yer boring me, shut up! This screen is giving me a headache.

Jimmy   Leave it. They'll be here soon.

Gina   He had better behave himself.

Jimmy   Who?

Gina   Lawrie.

Loud rap music coming from upstairs.

I don't believe him. (*Shouts.*) Glen! Turn it down. Glen! I tell you, I have had it with that bloody kid, he don't answer me no more!

Jimmy   I don't suppose that arsehole of a dad of his has bin to see him.

Gina   You taking the piss? Glen, I swear to fucking Christ!

Jimmy   Let me go.

Gina   What do you think I'm going to do?

Jimmy   I've seen the way you two have been at it lately.

Gina   Drag his arse down here.

Jimmy *goes upstairs to get* **Glen**. **Gina** *lights up a cigarette.* **Jimmy** *returns with* **Glen**, *fourteen and with an attitude.*

Glen   Yeah, wat?

Gina   You deaf?

Glen   No.

Gina   Bloody should be, shit you play.

Glen   Ain't shit.

Jimmy   I can't even understand half the things they're saying.

Glen   Ca you ain't wid it guy.

Gina   English, Glen, we speak English in here.

Glen *sucks his teeth.*

Gina   Excuse me, what was that?

Jimmy   Just tell me what you get from it.

Glen   Loads.

Gina   Yeah, like learning to call a woman a bitch.

Jimmy   You want to listen to music, Glen, the Kinks, Pink Floyd, the Who!

Glen   Who?

Jimmy   You taking the mick?

Glen   Old man.

Jimmy   Oi!

Gina   He ain't bin rude, Dad, he ends every sentence on 'man'. And you know why? Because he's been hanging round with them black kids from the estate, when I specifically told him not to.

Glen   I don't remember that.

Gina   Do not take the piss, Glen.

Glen   Dem boys are awright, Mum.

Gina   No they are not.

Jimmy   Yer mum's right, son, I've seen them, they'll get you in bother.

Gina   They have already. I had to go down his school again, him and his black mates were picking on sum little Asian kid.

Jimmy   What, him? You sure?

Gina   One more strike and he's out.

Glen   I weren't picking on him.

Gina   Not what the teacher said.

Jimmy *clips him on the head.*

Glen   Oi! Move, man!

Jimmy   Little kid thinks he's a hard man now eh? Picking on sum little Asian kid.

Glen   Mum?

Gina   Mum what?

Glen   Tell him.

Gina   You won't always have yer black mates backing you up, you know; one day, those Asian kids are gonna fight back. Prince Naseem was a little Asian kid once, look at him now.

Jimmy   Come on, take yer grandad on, if you think yer hard enuff.

Glen   Will you move from me please.

Gina   All right, Dad.

Jimmy   I hardly touched him.

Gina   It's enuff.

Jimmy   Little girl.

Gina   No more trouble, you hearing me?

Glen (*sees the fag in the ashtray*)   Was that you? Thought you quit.

Gina   I am addressing my addiction.

Glen   See her, Grandad, she fuckin goes on about me . . .

Gina   Oi, oi, less of the fuckin! If I want to have a smoke, I will have a smoke, so shut yer noise. The best thing you can do with temptation, is give in to it – Oscar Wilde.

Glen   Who dat, yer new boyfriend?

Gina   I don't even want to think about what they are not teaching you at school, I really don't. This whole area is going nowhere.

Glen's *mobile phone rings.*

Glen   Who dis? Awright, man, wass up? You joke! Is it! Nuh, man, wat? Yeah, I'm up fer it dread.

Gina *takes the phone off him.*

Glen   Giss it.

Gina (*to phone*)   Hello, this is Glen's mother speaking –

Glen   Mum, no.

Gina   I am afraid he cannot come to the phone, as he is in an awful lot of trouble, and will not be coming out, for the next twenty-five years, feel free to call back then. (*Hangs up.*)

Glen   Yer chat is dry.

Jimmy   What was that he was saying?

Gina   'Nuh, man!'

Jimmy   'Yeah, I'm up fer it dread!' (*Laughs.*)

Glen   You don't hang up on T like that.

Gina   Who?

Glen   T. Bad T.

Gina   Is that his name?

Glen   His street name.

Gina   Wass yer street name?

Glen   Ain't got one yet.

Gina   Ah! (*Pats his cheek.*)

Glen   I won't get it now, yer shamin me.

Jimmy   Yer little whiner.

Glen   I'm sorry.

Gina   Like you mean it!

Glen   SORRY!

Gina   Good.

She *pops her head round the other bar.*

Dad, go give Kelly a hand.

Jimmy   Ware you going?

Gina   Cellars.

Jimmy   Oi, Glenny boy.

Glen   Glen!

Jimmy   Don't get arsey with me, you little shit. Put these names on these seats. Some of the boys have reserved seats for the game.

Glen   Awright if I have a drink?

Jimmy   Yeah of course it is, don't be silly. (**Glen** *strolls to the bar.*) Get out of it! He only believed me. And don't even think about sneaking one away, cos I'll know.

Glen   Cool.

Jimmy *leaves.* **Glen** *pours himself a shot of whisky.* **Jimmy** *creeps up from behind, clips him round the ear, and takes the glass from him.*

Jimmy   Moby. (*Exits.*)

Glen *does as he is told, and puts down the stickers.* **Mark** (*black, early thirties*) *comes in.*

Glen   Awright, man?

Mark   Yeah.

Glen   Wass up?

Mark   What?

Glen   Nuttin.

Mark   Where's yer mum?

Glen   Cellar. Who are you?

Mark   Mark.

Glen   Mark who?

Mark   Juss Mark.

Glen   Awright man, easy guy!

His phone rings again.

(*Answers.*) Who dis? Awright, man. It was my mum weren't
it. She took it off me, wat was I supposed to do, lick her
down or summin? Yeah, so wass up? Wat now? Yeah, well
why didn't you, awright come in.

Two young black kids come in, **Bad T** *and* **Duane**. *They are the
same age as* **Glen**.

Duane   Yes, Glen!

Glen   Awright, man? T?

Bad T   Ware de booze, boy?

Glen   You mad?

Bad T   Did yu juss call me mad?

Glen   No.

Bad T   Did the boy juss call me mad, Duane?

Duane   Musta done! Cos I heard it.

Bad T   Lesson number one, don't ever call T mad, yeah.

Glen   Awright, I'm sorry.

Bad T   S'right. So pass the booze.

Glen   I can't, man.

Bad T   Did the boy jus say he can't, Duane?

Duane   Musta done, T, cos I heard it.

Bad T   Lesson number two, don't ever say you can't, yeah?

Glen   Yeah.

Bad T   Yeah wat?

Glen   Yeah watever, I'm sorry.

Bad T   Better.

Duane   The boy learnin, T. Awright, Mark?

Bad T   Come on, boy, booze! I want a Jack D and Coke.

Glen   My mum will go mad.

Bad T   Mad bitch. 'bout she chat to me like that on the phone.

Duane (*finds a picture of* **Gina** *behind the bar*)   Rah, is that her?

Glen   Yeah, she won, landlady of the year or summin.

Bad T   How much you have in this till?

Glen   T, don't man.

Bad T   Did the boy juss say don't T, Duane?

Duane (*laughing*)   Musta done, cos I heard it.

Bad T   Lesson number three, never say T don't man, yeah? Yeah? Come on?

Glen   Sorry.

Bad T   Good. I was joking anyway yer fool, chill.

Duane   Check his mum, man.

Bad T   Rah!

Duane   Ennit!

Bad T   This yer mum, boy? Fer trut?

Glen   Yeah.

Bad T   Rah!

Duane   Definitely.

Bad T   Definitely would!

Duane   Definitely!

Bad T   She like it on top, Glen?

Glen   Top of wat?

Duane *roars with laughter.*

Glen   Wat?

Bad T   She turn tricks, Glen? Yer mudda turn tricks? You know wat I mean by tricks don't yer?

Glen   Yeah.

Bad T   So, does yer mudda turn tricks?

Glen   Yeah, you mean like card tricks right?

Duane *and* **T** *carry on howling.*

Glen   Wat you saying about my mum, T?

Bad T   Nuttin, forget it, Glen, yer awright.

Duane (*looks at picture of* **Gina** *again*)   Hmmm, oh yes!

Bad T   Definitely!

Glen   Careful, man.

The boys glare at him.

My mum's in the cellar.

Bad T   Did the boy juss tell us to be careful?

Duane   Musta done, cos I . . .

Bad T   Lesson number four, never . . .

Glen   . . . Yeah, I'm sorry.

Bad T   You gotta learn to relax, bredren.

Duane   Ennit.

Bad T   So wat you say, Mark?

Mark   Nuttin. Yer the one doing all the talkin.

Duane   So wass up, Mark, how come you don't come round no more?

Mark   Ask yer mum.

Bad T   Wass this?

Duane   Went out wid my mum ennit.

Bad T   Yer mum's had nuff men.

Mark   You keeping out of trouble, Tyrone?

Bad T   T! Bad T!

Mark   Listen, I used to watch yer mudda change yer nappy, so don't even bother coming to me wid this Bad T business.

Bad T (*eyes* **Glen** *and* **Duane** *laughing*)   Wat you laughin at?

Duane   Nuttin, T.

Glen   Sorry, T.

Duane   You watchin the game today, T?

Bad T   I ain't watchin no rubbish English match. They lose at everyting.

Someone's phone goes off. All the boys reach for their pockets. But it is **Mark**'*s that is ringing.*

Mark   Sorry, boys. (*Answers.*) Hi, Karen, wass up? Nuh, he ain't here yet. I don't know, hold up a minute. (*Walks over to a discreet part of the bar.*) Yeah, go on.

Bad T   Rah, Glen, so thass yer phone?

Glen   Smart ennit?

Duane   Smarter than yours, T.

Bad T   Let me see. (*Examines it.*) It's light, wass the reception like?

Glen   Sharp.

Bad T   You get text yeah?

Glen   It's got everything. I can download e-mail, go on Internet and that. Free voicemail.

Duane   Nice, Glen.

Glen   I know.

Mark (*to phone*)   No, I'm stayin here till he comes. I'll come back wid him. How am I suppose to know that, I juss got here.

Bad T   It's so light.

Mark   Cos yer good wid him.

Bad T   Fits into my pocket nice.

Mark   Karen, please don't start, I beg you. I'll see you later.

Bad T   Don't mess up the lining or nuttin.

Glen   Told yer.

Bad T   Sell it to me.

Glen *laughs.*

Bad T   Sell it.

Glen   Nuh, man.

Bad T   Come on.

Glen   I don't want to sell it.

Bad T   Fifteen.

Glen   No.

Bad T   Twenty.

Duane   For that? It's worth twice that . . .

Bad T   You see me talking to you, Duane?

Glen   I don't want to sell it, T.

Bad T   Wat you gonna do wid a phone like this?

Glen   Ring people and that.

Duane   Give the boy back his phone, man.

Bad T   Yeah, but it's too nice fer a white boy like him to have, best let me have it, someone who appreciates it. Look, the fool ain't even got no numbers in his phone book.

Glen   I only bought it the other day.

Bad T   Glen, has anyone, anyone at all, rang you on the phone, besides me?

Glen   No.

Bad T   Anyone ask fer yer number?

Glen   No.

Bad T   So why you reach for it, when Mark's phone rang then?

Glen   I dunno, I juss thought . . .

Bad T   You thought wat, Glen?

Glen   I dunno, juss thought.

Bad T   I'm surprised yer brain can even do that, you thick cunt!

Duane   T man!

Bad T   So much you sellin it to me, Glen?

Glen   Nuttin.

Bad T   Nuttin, you giving it to me fer nuttin, cheers.

Glen   Hold up.

Bad T   Nice.

Glen   I don't wanna sell it.

Bad T   Twelve quid.

Glen   You said twenty a minute ago.

Bad T   Every time you say no, the price goes down. You got a nice jacket too.

Duane   T?

Bad T   Glen?

Glen   I ain't sellin it.

Bad T   Nine.

Glen   I can't.

Bad T   Eight.

Glen   I saved fer months to get it.

Bad T   Six. Keep whining, Glen. You crying now?

Glen   No.

Bad T   Fucking boy's crying, man.

Glen   I ain't.

Bad T   White boy love to cry, ennit, Duane?

Mark   Give the boy back his phone.

Bad T   Excuse me?

Mark   No, excuse you, give the boy back his phone Tyrone.

Bad T   The name's T, right.

Mark   Fuck wat yer name is, give the boy back his phone.

Bad T   Here. (*Hands it back.*) Tek yer fuckin phone. (*To* **Duane**.) And you defendin him.

Duane   All I said was . . .

Bad T   Ca you love the white, man. You want suck him off, ennit? (*To* **Glen**.) It was a joke, Glen, I was jokin wid you. You shouldn't carry on so, someone might juss come and tief up yer life, never mind yer mobile phone.

Gina *comes back to find* **Bad T** *and* **Duane** *behind her bar.*

Gina   Well, make yerself at home, why don't yer? And you are?

Glen   Duane and T.

Gina   Oh, so yer Bad T?

Bad T   I'm big too. (*He and* **Duane** *laugh.*)

Gina   So wat are Duane, and Big T, doing behind my bar? Come on, move, out!

Bad T   You mind?

Gina   No.

Bad T   Don't touch wat you can't afford.

Gina   Is that right?

Bad T   Ennit.

Gina   I will do more than touch, little boy, if you don't shift, never mind ennit.

Duane *and* **T** *ogle over her again.*

Duane   Oh yeah.

Bad T   Definitely.

Gina   You wish.

Bad T   When you lass have black in you?

Mark   Hey!

Gina   Is that supposed to make me quiver?

Mark   Tek yer friend and go home, Tyrone.

Bad T   You my dad?

Mark   No, but I can call him. Do you want him chasin you round the estate wid his leather belt again?

Bad T (*sees* **Duane** *giggling*)   Wat you laughin at? Come!

Duane   Later, Glen.

Bad T   Yeah go kiss yer wife goodbye!

Glen   Hold up.

Bad T   Well come now, if yer comin.

Gina   Ware do you think yer going?

Glen   Yer shamin me, Mum.

Gina   I'll do more than shame yer, if you step one foot out of that door.

Glen   I won't be late.

Gina   You won't be back at all.

Glen   Later. (*Leaves.*)

Gina   He don't listen to a word I say. Like I ain't here. Fuckin kids.

Mark   That Tyrone come juss like his dad, too much mout.

Gina   So?

Mark   So?

Gina   What about you?

Mark   Nuttin.

Gina   How you doing, gorgeous?

Mark   Awright.

Gina   Thought you didn't drink in here no more.

Mark   I thought I'd slum it.

Gina   Cheeky sod. You on leave?

Mark   No I'm out.

Gina   Wat, for good?

Mark   So that was little Glen?

Gina   Little cunt more like. He wants a slap. How's yer dad, Mark?

Mark   So-so.

Gina   I used to see him all the time down the high street, coming out of the betting shop, he would always call me over, sayin hello and that, askin if I have a boyfriend yet.

Mark   Yer still look good, Gina.

Gina   Yeah, yeah.

Mark   You still love to put yerself down. Didn't you see the way those boys were lookin at yer? Yer fit, gal, deal wid it.

Gina   I know someone who will be very pleased to see you.

Mark   No don't.

Gina   Shut up. (*Calls.*) Dad! In here a minute, I got a surprise.

Mark   Oh, look at the time.

Gina   Sit! Dad!

Jimmy Wat?

Gina In here. Fuckin 'ell.

Jimmy (*approaching*) Wat?

Gina Look.

Jimmy Marky boy! How you doin, you awright, son?
You look it.

Mark Cheers, Jimmy.

Jimmy Still playing footie, I hope. Pub team are playing
this mornin.

Mark Yeah?

Jimmy I still remember when you played for us, blindin
he was, blindin! Everyone still talks about that goal you got
against the Stag's Head: he ran with it, one end of the pitch
to the other he was, no lie. He pissed on that goal Ryan
Giggs got for Man U against Arsenal, pissed on it, well and
truly pissed on it!

Gina Yeah, Dad, cheers. Punters!

Jimmy We'll talk sum more in a minute, son, you
watchin the game?

Mark Na.

Jimmy Na!

Mark I dunno.

Jimmy Behave yerself.

Mark We'll see.

Jimmy Gina, buy him a drink on me. (*Leaves.*)

Gina Yes, sir!

Mark He ain't changed.

Gina So, Mark?

Mark   Yes, Gina?

Gina   We gonna talk about what happened, or are you juss gonna sit there wid yer gob open?

Mark   Let's not. I'm juss looking for my brother, I heard he drinks in here now.

Gina   I was wondering how long it would be before you came back. You see the door? Well, keep yer eyes on it, our pub team will be back any sec. He plays for them. You know he looks juss like you.

Doors swing open. **Lawrie**, **Lee**, *followed by* **Becks** *come in. They do not look happy.*

Gina   Oh shit. Well, come on, how bad was it.

Lawrie   We stuffed the bastards!

The lads cheer.

Boys (*singing*)   Cheer up Duke of Yorks, oh what can it mean, to a, fat landlord bastard, and a, shit football team. (*Chants.*) King George, King George . . .

Gina   You tellin me you useless bastards won?

Becks   3–fuckin–2!

Gina   Oi, Dad, they only bloody won!

Lee   Set 'em up, Gina.

Lawrie   Oh yes, nuttin more sexier than a landlady pouring a smooth top.

Gina   Don't get out much, do yer, Lawrie?

Lawrie   I'll show yer wat I can get out.

Lee   Oi, behave yerself.

Gina   Like I'll be able to see it.

Becks   Nice one, Gina.

Lawrie   Kiss her arse while yer at it.

Gina   Well come on then, blow by blow.

Lawrie   Played them off the field, Gina, gave 'em a fuckin lesson in football.

Becks   Fat cunts.

Lee   It's funny how those fat cunts were 2–0 up.

Lawrie   Only cos of him, I coulda driven a bus through the amount of space he give 'em. Wants shooting.

Becks   Fuck off, Lawrie.

Lawrie   Oooh! You shoulda seen the looks on their faces at half-time, Gina, every one of them, looking like their case was about to come up. Right, thass it I thought, time for my pep talk. I rounded them all up, like this see. (*Demonstrates using* **Lee** *and* **Becks**.) I goes, listen to me, listen to me! Passion! I wanna see some passion. We gotta help each other out, this is no good, we gotta learn to pass to each other, keep control of the ball! (*Screams.*) Look at me! Ain't we?

Lee/Becks   Yeah!

Lawrie   Who are yer?

Lee/Becks   The George.

Lawrie   Who are yer?

Lee/Becks   The George!

Lawrie   Thank you! Well, that was it then, second half, different story. I was going, keep back, keep back, chase, chase, keep the ball, keep the ball –

Lee   Thought he was gonna lose his voice.

Becks   I prayed he would lose his voice.

Lawrie   When Lee got the ball, I tell yer, I heard music, Gina. I goes to him.

Lee   Screaming down my ear he was.

Lawrie   Yer tart! I goes, go on, broth, give it a good spin, he places it right into the back, the goalie didn't know wat day it was. Coulda kissed him.

Lee   You did.

Lawrie *kisses him again.*

Gina   Who got the other two?

Lawrie   The black kid, wasshisface?

Becks   Barry. Useful, weren't he, Lawrie?

Lawrie   Yeah, he was good, the boy done good.

Becks   He did more than good, he won the game for us.

Lee   Good penalty taker.

Becks   Wicked player.

Lawrie   Wicked player? Listen to him, trying to sound like a brother.

Becks   I'm juss sayin, he won the game for us.

Lawrie   Yeah I know wat he did, he's a wicked player, as you so delicately put it. But it was a team effort. He didn't juss win it by himself.

Becks   Might as well have.

Lawrie   You married to the cunt or wat? The boy did good, no need to break out into a song about it. Worry about yer own football, never mind droolin over wasshisface.

Becks   You callin me queer?

Lawrie   You got summin to hide, precious?

Gina   Ladies?

Becks   So wat about you, taking a swing at their captain.

Lawrie   Weren't my fault.

Becks Nor was the goal.

Lee Will you two lovebirds shut up.

Lawrie That ref was a knob.

Becks Now thass true.

Lawrie That captain of theirs was committing untold fouls, not once did he get his book out.

Lee Till you opened yer mouth.

Gina What did he say?

Lawrie Only the truth.

Lee Don't tell her.

Lawrie I accused him of not wanting to book one of his own.

Lee Arsehole.

Lawrie Cheers, broth.

Lee I meant you.

Lawrie Don't tell me you weren't thinkin it an'all.

Becks It's true. I saw them havin a right old chat afterwards.

Lawrie They love stickin together them lot.

Gina Let me guess, the ref was black?

Lawrie As soot. Never seen anything so dark.

Lee Hold it down.

Lawrie Awright, Mark? Long time no see. Still giving it large in Paddy Land? He lose his tongue or what?

Gina Behave.

Lawrie Only askin.

Gina You've asked.

Lawrie   You know me, Gina, keep the peace.

Gina   Yeah.

Lee   She knows yer.

Lawrie   Got our seats, Gina?

Gina   Have a look.

Lawrie   Oh wass this, you put us at the back.

Gina   Jason asked first.

Lawrie   Fuck that. (*He swaps seats.*) You don't mind, do yer?

Gina   Any trouble, it's you I'm comin for.

Lawrie (*clicks on the remote, picture is blue*)   Gina, wass this, it's all blue.

Gina   Ask yer thievin mate over there.

Lawrie   Becks! You fuckin . . .

Becks   It was workin all right when I sold it to them.

Lawrie (*throws the remote at him*)   Fix it!

Lee   So how you doing, Mark?

Mark   Lee.

Lee   You on leave?

Mark   I quit.

Lee   You joke?

Mark   I had enuff.

Lee   You!

Mark   Yep.

Lee   How's yer dad?

Mark   Up and down . . . Heard about yours. Sorry, yeah.

Lee   S'right. Look, listen, yeah . . .

Mark   Don't.

Lee   Mark . . .

Mark   Don't.

Lawrie   Lee, over here a sec.

Lee   Wat?

Lawrie   Nuttin.

Lee   So wat you callin me for?

Lawrie   Geezer don't wanna know, mate.

Gina (*to* **Becks**)   Wat you fuckin done now?

Becks   I'm adjusting.

Gina   It's black an'white. Juss give us some colour.

Becks   Awright, don't get out of yer pram over it. You reckon we'll win, Lawrie?

Lawrie   We better, restore some pride after that fuck-up in Belgium. I mean, how fuckin bad was that? The nation that gave the world football. (*Roars.*) Come on, you England!

Becks   Come on, England!

Lee   Come on!

Lawrie   2002, boys, make it happen.

Gina   Becks, Becks, stop!

Becks   Wat?

Gina   Weren't you watchin? You had it, picture, it was perfect, colour and everything, go back.

Becks *presses the remote.*

Gina   It's turned blue again.

Becks   Hold up.

The menu comes up on the screen.

Wass this?

Lawrie   It's the menu. Yer pressin the wrong button, you muppet.

Lee   Hold up, Becks?

Becks   Wat now?

Lee   Don't get arsey, I'm tryin to help you here.

Becks   Wat?

Lee   Go to services, on yer right.

Becks   I know.

Lee   Well, go on then.

Becks   Right.

Lee   Click on that. Now, scroll down to picture settings. Click on that. Contrast. Go up.

Gina   Yer going down, he said up.

Lawrie   Prat.

Lee   Up, up.

Becks   I'm going up.

Lee   Awright, yeah thass it, stop! That'll do.

Lawrie   Finally.

Gina   Thank you, Constable.

Lee   Pleasure to be of service, Madam.

Gina   It's good to have someone here with brains.

Becks   Hey, wass keepin them?

Lawrie   They'll be here. Alan won't miss the kick-off, trust me.

Lee   You invited Alan?

Lawrie   Yeah.

Becks   I saw yer mate Darren, Lawrie, going into one about not getting a ticket for the game. Geezer's off his head. He reckons he's gonna stand outside Wembley, give the Germans some verbal. Take them on like he did in Charleroi.

Lawrie   He shat himself in Charleroi. Ran back to the hotel before it all kicked off. It was me giving them Germans some gyp.

Lee   I didn't hear that, did I?

Lawrie   Of course not, Constable.

Becks   What you do?

Lawrie   Wat do you think? We gave them a right spanking. We were in this caff, watching the game. One–nil up right.

Becks (*chants*)   Shearer!

Lawrie   Right, shut up. There was this couple of Krauts sitting nearby, so juss for a laugh, I goes, I gives the old Nazi salute, going like this I was. Fuckin ages I was at it, till finally I catches one of dem giving me the eyeball, I ask wat his problem was, he goes all menstrual, going on about cos they're Germans, it don't make them Nazis, blah, blah, bloody blah! I goes, awright, mate, calm yerself, you a Jew or wat?

Becks *laughs out loud.*

Lawrie   Next minute, the cunt's comin at me comin at me wid a beer bottle. Tiny little cunt he was an'all. I goes, give us that, behave yerself. I take the bottle right off him, give him a slap, stamped on his fuckin head, shoulda seen it, I lean down to him, I goes, Do I take it that yer not a Jew then?

Lee   I didn't hear that, I am so not here.

Mark   You ain't changed.

Lawrie   Did he juss say summin?

Lee   No.

Lawrie   Oi, Mark, you say summin, mate? Mark? You found yer tongue then? Oi?

Lee   Lawrie.

Lawrie   I heard him say summin.

Lee   No you didn't. Let's play.

Lawrie   Have a day off, will yer? Yer off duty.

Gina   Listen to the policeman, Lawrence.

Lawrie   Awright. Well, put the money in.

The boys head for the table football, **Lee** *puts fifty pence in, a ball comes out. The brothers play against each other.*

Becks   Do you know if Rob got a ticket for the match, Lawrie?

Lawrie   He said he'd try. Bastard!

Lee   It's all in the wrist!

Becks   I thought I juss saw his face in the crowd, one of the cameras whizzed by, I'm sure it was him.

Lawrie   Yeah? Give us a shout when you see him next. Oh wat?

Lee   Skill, mate.

Becks   You want to play doubles?

Lawrie   Fuck off, yer worse than me.

Becks   Come on.

Lawrie   Ask our West Indian friend over there.

Becks (*to* **Mark**)   You fancy a game, Mark?

Lee   Leave him alone, Becks.

Mark   Yeah, come, why not.

Becks   I got a partner.

Lawrie   Wat do you want me to do, sing? So, Marcus?

Mark   Mark.

Lawrie   How confident are yer?

Lee   Wat you doing?

Mark *throws down forty quid.*

Mark   This much? Best out of three?

Lee   Mark, don't.

Mark   You my dad?

Lawrie   Exactly, Mark, pay no attention to the old woman. Becks?

Becks   I'm short.

Mark   Don't worry about it.

Becks   Cheers, mate.

Lawrie   Let's play ball.

Mark   You gonna cover the bet?

Lawrie   Lee?

Lee   Oh bloody hell, Lawrie.

Lawrie   Come on.

Lee   Do I look like a cashpoint?

Lawrie   All I got is ten.

Lee   Yer a pain in the arse.

Lawrie   Come on.

Lee   Every time I see you, you cost me money.

Lawrie   Broth? Brother!

Lee   You juss don't listen. (*Gives him thirty.*) You ain't even listening now.

Lawrie   Wat? Joke. Come here. (*Kisses him on the head.*)

Lee   Get off me. I hate it when you do that.

Lawrie   Love yer! Gina, my love, bank this for us, will yer. Let's play ball! Mark, my boy, would you care to kick off.

Mark   No you can.

Lawrie   No yer awright, go ahead.

Mark   I said I'm awright.

Lawrie   Come on.

Mark   You start.

Lee   Will somebody.

Lawrie   Yer missin the point here, Mark.

Mark   Which is what?

Lawrie   You see, this here is my pub, my home from home as it were. You are a guest, I am the host, extending my hospitality.

Mark   I don't want it.

Lee   Fuck's sake, I'll do it.

Lee *drops the ball, they all play.* **Lee** *scores.*

Lawrie   Yes!

Becks   Shit, sorry.

Mark   Don't worry.

Mark *plays the ball. He plays like a lunatic, he is too fast for* **Lawrie** *and* **Lee** *and scores.*

Mark   Yes!

Lawrie   Right, come on, Lee.

Lee *drops the ball in,* **Mark** *is just as fast, if not faster, he scores again.*

Becks   Yes!

Lawrie   Shit. Come on, Lee.

Lee   Awright!

Lee *drops the ball again.* **Mark** *is playing like a maniac now.* **Becks** *just stops and stands back and watches him.* **Mark** *scores.*

Mark   Oh yes!

Lawrie   Bollocks!

Becks   Does it hurt being that good, Mark?

Mark   Torture. Cheers, Gina. (*Collects the money from her.*)

Lawrie   You knew he was useful.

Lee   I knew you wouldn't listen.

Mark   Another please, Gina.

Gina   So you still here?

Mark   Till I see my brother.

Gina   Jimmy will be pleased.

Lee   Still practising?

Mark   Another time, Lee.

Lee   She dumped me as well, you know.

Mark   I don't care about that.

Lee   Sod yer then.

Mark   Right on.

Door opens. **Phil**, **Jason** *and* **Alan** *enter, loud cheering, singing, except* **Alan**, *who walks in coolly, standing between them.* **Lawrie**, **Becks** *and* **Lee** *join their mates in the singing.*

Boys   We're on our way, we are Kev's twenty-two, hear the roar, of the red, white and blue, this time, more than any other, this time, we're gonna find a way, find a way to get it on, time, to get it on together.

Gina   Shall we keep it down, gents? Hi, Phil.

Phil   Awright, Gina.

Gina   So how's life in Watford?

Phil   Sweet as.

Becks   He'll be following their team next.

Phil   Bollocks.

Becks   Giving Elton John a tug.

Phil   Shut it, Becks.

Boys (*sing*)   Don't sit down, with Elton around, or you might get a penis up yer arse!

Gina   Now, now, boys, not in front of the lady.

Alan   It's all right, Gina, I'll keep them in line. (*To screen.*) Come on, lads, got a lot of living up to do.

Phil   We had 'em in June.

Alan   Romania had us in June.

Boys (*sing*)   Come on England, come on England, come on England, let's have another win.

Alan   Where's yer dad?

Gina (*shouts*)   Dad? Like yer haircut, Phil.

Phil   Yeah?

Gina   Yeah, very David Beckham. Suits yer.

*The boys start teasing **Phil** regarding **Gina**.*

Phil   Behave yerselves.

Becks (*watching the screen*)   Commentary's started.

Jason (*roars*) Come on, lads.

Phil   Come on, you England!

Lawrie *and* **Lee** *join in the roar.* **Jimmy** *appears to get some crisps.*

Jimmy   Wat?

Gina   Yer little friend's here.

Jimmy   Awright, Alan?

Alan   James. Watchin the game?

Jimmy   Be right wid yer, juss serving.

Alan   Lawrie my boy. Good result today, well played.

Lawrie   You remember my kid brother Lee.

Alan   The policeman, you all right, son?

Lee   Yep.

Alan   Spitting image of yer old man, you are. Still a PC?

Lawrie   Detective constable now, if you don't mind, movin to Sutton.

Lee   Lawrie.

Lawrie   Shut up, I don't know why yer keepin it a secret, I'm proud of yer. I kept tellin him it would work out for him, but he never believes me. The state he was in last year.

Alan   State?

Lawrie   Got stabbed.

Alan   Nasty.

Lawrie   Yeah, some coon. It happened at a rave, weren't it, Lee?

Lee   Will you shut up.

Lawrie   He didn't hear, like I care.

Alan   Easy, son.

Boys (*chant*)   ENGLAND, ENGLAND, ENGLAND . . .

Becks   Come on, Rob, ware are yer?

Jason   Wat is he there?

Becks   He was in the crowd a second ago.

Phil   How did he get in? He's banned from every ground in the country.

Lawrie   You think that'll stop Rob? They tried to stop us going into France for '98, we were there though, despite all the efforts and a huge operation by the boys in blue to keep us away. Ooops, sorry, Lee, you didn't hear that. We were there though, oh we were so there.

Jason   You there when the trouble kicked off?

Lawrie   The second Batty missed that penalty, I knew it was gonna kick off. It was fuckin war on the streets. Argies, Krauts, coppers, didn't fuckin matter. We were England!

Alan   Thinking went right out of the window.

Lawrie   Least we were winnin that one.

Alan   You got arrested and thrown in a French cell, you daft sod. Never fight a battle you can't win.

Jason   Wat was Batty doin taking a penalty anyhow?

Mark   Jase?

Jason   Awright, Mark?

Mark   Where's my brother? He was playin today?

Alan   You're Barry's brother?

Mark   Yes.

Alan   You should be proud of him, that boy is useful.

Mark   He ain't a boy.

Alan   Easy.

Mark   Where is he?

Jason   He walked.

Mark   While you all drove?

Alan   There wasn't enough room. I had a lot of stuff in the back. I'm a painter and decorator. It was hard getting those two muppets in. We drew straws.

Mark   And he got the short one.

Alan   Yes, he did. What's his problem?

Mark   You can talk to me.

Alan   No need to fly off, son.

Mark   Where's my brother?

Barry *comes in, dancing and singing (New Order's 'World in Motion'); he makes a right show of it, parading himself in front of the lads who are egging him on.* **Barry** *has the flag of St George painted all over his face.*

Barry *(singing)*   You've got to hold or kick, and do it at the right time, you can be slow or fast, but you must get to the line, they'll always hit you and hurt you, defend or attack, there's only one way to beat them, get round the back, catch me if you can, cos I'm the England man, wat yer lookin at, is the master plan, we better move with pace, this is a football song, three lions on my chest, I know we can't go wrong! We're singin for England . . .

Boys   EN-GER-LAND! We're singin the song, We're singin for England, EN-GER-LAND, Arrivederci, it's one on one! We're singin for England, EN-GER-LAND . . .

Phil   Barry, over here!

Barry *goes over to the boys. One by one they take turns rubbing or kissing his bald head.*

Barry   Anyone else?

Alan   Yeah, over here, boy . . . (*Rubs his head.*)

Phil   Good boy.

Jason   Fuckin won it for us.

Barry   Thank you, thank you, thank you – (*Sees* **Mark**.) Awright, broth?

Mark   Can I talk to you?

Barry   Game's gonna start.

Mark   Won't take long.

Jason   Got yer seat here, Baz.

Barry   Cheers, Jase.

The teams line up to hear the national anthems. The German one plays first. The lads boo and jeer.

Boys (*to the tune of 'Go West'*)   Stand up, if you won the war! Stand up, if you won the war, stand up, if you won the war . . .

Gina   Feet off the seats, if you please.

The English national anthem is played. The boys sing along. Some jump on the table, **Gina** *protests. They all cheer at the end. The boys then cheer and applaud as each player is called on the TV screen. They do the same when the German team is read out, only this time they jeer.*

Boys (*chant*)   ENGLAND! ENGLAND! ENGLAND!

Alan   Come on, lads.

Lawrie   Let's fuckin have some!

Alan   Lawrence? About wat we spoke about, yer in.

Lawrie   Cheers.

Lee (*approaching*)   Wat was that?

Lawrie   Nosy.

Game kicks off. Boys cheer and applaud.

Mark   Barry?

Barry   Later, Mark, come on, pull up a chair.

Phil   You tell him, boy.

Mark (*grabs him*)   Come here!

Barry   Hey!

Mark   Excuse us!

Mark *ushers his brother into the Gents where they start to bicker.*

Becks   Wass up there?

Lawrie   Must be a black thing.

Becks   Two black geezers in the Gents, dodgy.

Lee   Shut up, Becks.

Becks   Joke.

Phil   Come on, you England!

*The boys join **Phil**'s roar. Lights up on the Gents.*

Barry   I'm missin the start here.

Mark   Wat was that? Dancin like sum spaz, lettin them rub yer head like a genie's lamp.

Barry   They do it at every match, for luck. It's a laugh.

Mark   Wipe that shit off yer face.

Barry   Don't come down here and start, Mark.

Mark   You think I'm here by choice? I feel ill juss bein here. I can't wait to go home so I can have a wash.

Barry   Go home then.

Mark   All this, 'Leave it out, mate, you know wat I mean, I'm a geezer ain't I' –

Barry   Let me watch the match!

Mark   Karen said you ain't bin home fer weeks, wass that about? Too busy to see yer own dad?

Barry   You come to take me back?

Mark   He's askin for yer.

Barry   I ain't seein him.

Mark   Show sum respect.

Barry   For that mess that lies in bed all day? That ain't my dad, why can't he hurry up and die?

Mark   Fuckin little . . .

Barry   Karen feels the same way, you as well. You love to act high and mighty now yer back; where were you when he was gettin sick?

Mark   Look, let's chat when we get home, yeah?

Barry   I'm watchin the game.

Mark   Ware you get that cut on yer neck?

Barry   Romanian fan. Charleroi.

Mark   You were at Charleroi? Fuck's sake.

Barry   Shoulda seen wat I did to him. (*Demonstrates.*) Glassed him right up.

Mark   Why don't you get a tattoo of the Union Jack while yer at it.

Barry *rolls up his shirt. He has a tattoo of the British Bulldog on his lower back.*

Barry   I didn't even pass out. Almost as good as yours, I reckon.

Mark   Wat are you doin to yerself?

Barry   Nuttin you wouldn't do, once.

Mark   I don't want Dad going thru this shit again.

Barry   Fuck off back to the army.

Mark   I'm outta the army, little man, for good.

Barry   Lose yer bottle again, Mark?

Mark   Yer comin home.

Barry   No.

Mark   I'll follow you all day if I have to.

Barry   Do it.

Mark   Kid . . .

Barry   I ain't a fuckin kid no more! You don't understand!

Mark   I don't understand?

Barry   I'm missin it.

Mark   You think yer a badman now, cos yu've had a couple of rucks, kicked a few heads? You've got no idea, son. When yer all alone with a gang of them, havin to fight 'em off by yourself, getting the shit kicked outta yer for yer trouble, you get back to me. It's bollocks, kid. It's their bollocks.

The boys stamp on the floor as they chant to the theme tune of The Great Escape. **Barry** *leaves the loo to watch the match with his mates. He joins in with the chant. The screen turns blue again. The boys protest.*

Gina   Becks, you stupid . . .

Becks   I'll fix it.

Gina   Keep yer bloody hands off.

Lee   Giss it.

Lawrie   Come on, broth.

Lee   Shut up.

Lee *sorts out the contrast. The colour picture comes back. The boys applaud.*

Phil   Nice.

Becks   Juss needs a bit of TLC now and then.

Gina   I want my money back.

Phil   Come on, England!

Boys (*chant*)   ENGLAND! ENGLAND! ENGLAND! . . .

Beck (*mocks*)   Southgate in the middle though.

Phil   When did Cole score last?

Mark   When did he last get a full game?

Gina (*approaching*)   Come on, boys, bunch up.

The boys get all excited by **Gina** *joining them. Cheers, wolf whistles, etc.*

Gina   All barks, no bites. You stayin then, Mark?

Mark   Yeah. Might as well.

Jason   Lampard should be playing.

Phil   An 'ammer playing, behave yerself.

Jimmy   Shut yer hole, Philip. You juss bring on yer bloody Chelsea at Upton Park next week, you'll bloody know it then.

Mobile phone rings. It's **Becks**'s.

Becks (*answers*)   Hello. Awright, Rob!

Jason (*shouts*)   Robbie, yer cunt!

Lawrie   Yer wanker!

Becks   Yer hear that? I said did yer hear that?

Lawrie   Ware is he? (*Shouts.*) Ware are yer, yer cunt!

Becks   He's there!

Jason   Wembley?

Becks   Yes, Jase, fuckin Wembley! (*To phone.*) Wat now?
He goes, there's a camera comin into view, he's gonna wave
at us.

Phil   He's there, fuckin 'ell!

They all cheer and wave.

Becks   We see yer, yer there.

They all see Rob from the screen, the boys scream and cheer louder.
Phil *pulls his trousers down and moons at the screen.*

Becks   Rob, Phil is only showin you his arse.

Gina (*to* **Jimmy**)   No trouble eh?

Jimmy   Philip, no more arse!

The boys roar with laughter as they see Rob mooning back at them.

Lawrie   He's only moonin back at us!

Jason   Yer wanker!

Becks   Ring me at half-time, yer nutter!

Lawrie   I tell yer, if we lose again, it's gonna kick off in
there.

Kelly (*off*)   Jimmy?

Jimmy   Kelly needs some help, Gina.

Gina   You better get back there.

Jimmy (*shouts*)   I'll be there in a sec.

Gina   Dad?

Jimmy   Fuck's sake!

The boys laugh as **Jimmy** *has to leave.*

Yeah, yeah, up yours.

Becks   Germans playing three at the back?

Barry   Looks like it.

Jason   Yes, come on, Owen.

Becks   Fuck!

Lee   Good run though.

Barry   He's a fast one.

Alan   Yeah, but then he lost it.

Jason   Nice one, Adams, make him eat dirt.

Lawrie   He's given away a free kick, yer sap.

Phil   Watch the post, watch the fuckin post!

Jason   Good one, Le Saux.

Becks   Doin summin right for once.

Jason   Leave him.

Becks (*acting camp*)   Oooh! (*Blows* **Jason** *a kiss.*)

Jason   Fuck off.

Gina   Nice control by Cole eh?

Lawrie   Yeah, but he's all mouth, no delivery him.

Mark   Cos no one gives him a chance.

Lawrie   Cos he never fuckin scores.

Mark   Shearer played nine games without scoring for England, nine! Didn't stop Venables pickin him.

Lawrie   Cole ain't Shearer.

Mark   He's never bin given a chance to be Shearer.

Barry   Lawrie's right.

Mark   Wat you know?

Barry   Watch him. He needs three or four chances to score a goal, Shearer only needed one.

Mark   He got forty-one goals in one season when he was with Newcastle, how many's he put in for Man U? War'do you want? Since when is a striker judged on how many chances he gets, leave me alone.

Phil   Southgate, you useless piece of shit.

Jason *takes out horn and blows on it, everyone jumps.*

Becks   Jase!

Phil   'kin 'ell.

Jason   Juss tryin to whip up a bit of excitement.

Gina   I'll whip it up yer arse.

Alan   Nice one, Scholes.

Lawrie   Come on, Scholes.

Barry   Get it up.

They sigh as Scholes loses the ball to German player Ballack. Scholes tugs him, Ballack falls. Free kick.

Becks   Wat!

Phil   Hamman won't score.

Barry   He plays for Liverpool ennit.

Hamman shoots from the free kick. He scores. German fans cheer. The boys are stunned.

Phil   Oh wat!

Jason   Nice one, Baz, yer jinxed it.

Barry   Move.

Jason   He did.

Lee   Wat difference it makes, he still scored.

Lawrie   Fuck off Voller, you German cunt!

Boys (*chant*) YER DIRTY GERMAN BASTARD! YER DIRTY GERMAN BASTARD!

Lawrie   Jase, ring Rob, tell him to give one of them Krauts a slap from me.

Alan   There's no point in taking it out on them.

Lawrie   Oh come on.

Alan   We should have had a red shirt in front of the ball. It weren't a strong kick, Seaman should have got that. A blind man could have got that.

Barry   We were well asleep at the back. Hamman saw a chance, he took it.

Alan   Too right he took it. The boy's right.

Phil   Check Keegan's face.

Becks   Yeah, you better be worried.

Jason   He was never cut out to be manager.

Barry   Ain't wat you said when he got the job, going on about him being the people's choice.

Jason   I never said that –

Barry   Lie!

Gina   Can we not bury them yet please.

England are awarded a free kick. Beckham lines up to take it.

Lee   Oh yes!

Lawrie   Come on, Beckham.

Phil   Get it in the box, please.

Jason   Let's have some more reds in there!

Barry   And leave them well exposed at the back, good call, Jase.

Jason   Piss off, Barry.

Barry   Ooh, handbag.

Jason   Scores a couple this mornin, and he thinks he's the dog's bollocks.

Beckham crosses the ball. It's headed back.

Gina   Get it back. And Philip?

Philip   Yeah?

Gina   Stop lookin at my tits.

The boys laugh as they tease **Phil**, *calling him a pervert, etc.*

Phil   I weren't.

Jimmy (*approaching*)   How goes it?

Becks   Phil's bin looking at Gina's tits.

Phil   I weren't, Jimmy, I swear to God.

Jimmy   You'll be prayin to God for your life, mate, if you step out – (*Sees.*) Oh Jesus. One–nil!

Mark   Hamman scored a blinder.

Lawrie   You a Kraut-lover now?

Alan   Easy, Lawrence.

Lawrie   It was a poxy free kick.

Mark   Watever.

Lawrie   No watever about it, boy.

Mark   Shut yer hole.

Lawrie   Shut my what, wass he say?

Lee   Yer missin the match.

Gina   Are we happy over there?

Lawrie   Sweet as.

Gina   Good.

Germans are on the attack, Bierhof is passed the ball. He is in an excellent position to score.

Becks Shit.

Jason Flag's up.

Barry Offside!

Phil Come on, England!

Jimmy They wanna stop playin wid themselves!

Cole has the ball, he makes a run.

Phil Come on, Cole.

Jason Yes.

Barry Free kick.

Jason Which cunt got him?

Gina Rehmar. Do you know any other words apart from cunt, Jase?

Beckham lines up for another free kick.

Alan Come on, Beckham.

Gina I don't care how he talks, he is gorgeous.

Jason He'll score.

Barry Got a crystal ball, Jase?

Beckham shoots, he misses.

You were sayin?

Jason It was on target.

Barry Yeah, look on the bright side.

Jason Wass yer problem?

Barry I'm havin a laugh.

Jason Leave it out.

Barry Or wat?

Gina Girls!

Lawrie Come on, Owen!

Alan Ooh, unlucky, son.

Phil That fuckin coach of theirs looks like Terry McDermott.

Jimmy He was a good player that Voller.

Alan How many goals he got when he was playin, Jimmy?

Jimmy 'bout forty-seven. Class player.

Lawrie For a Kraut.

Alan Nothing wrong with admiring the enemy once in a while.

Phil Come on, boys.

Barry England!

Jason They wanna take fucking Cole off.

Mark Why?

Jason Ain't pullin his weight.

Mark He ain't alone.

Jason I'm juss stating my opinion.

Mark Funny how he's the only black player on the pitch.

The boys protest at that remark.

Gina Come off it, Mark.

Mark All I said, it was funny.

Jason If thass wat I meant, that's wat I woulda said.

Mark Why him?

Jason He's playin shit.

Barry Yer talkin shit.

Mark Thank you.

Barry   Both of yer.

Mark   Hey, easy.

Jason   Paranoia.

Mark   I'm done.

Mark *goes to the Gents,* **Lee** *follows.*

Lawrie   Ware you going?

Jason   Wass yer brother's problem? He sayin I'm a racist?

Barry   I don't know wat he's doing.

Jason   Wanker.

Lights on in the Gents.

Lee   You don't even like Andy Cole. You told me once, you can't fart loud enough to describe how much you hate Man U, and anyone who plays for them.

Mark   Is it?

Lee   So wat gives? Did you hear that the Post Office recalled their Man U treble commemorative stamps, people couldn't figure out which side to spit on? Wat do Man U fans use for birth control? Their personalities. A man meets up with his mate and sees that his car is a total write-off, all covered with leaves, grass, branches, dirt and blood. He asks his mate, wat happened to yer car? The friend replies, well, I ran over David Beckham. Bloke goes, that explains the blood, but what about the leaves, the grass, and branches and dirt. The geezer says . . .

Mark   . . . he tried to escape runnin by through the park.

Mark *tries hard not to laugh, but gives in a little.. He then heads out.*

Lee   So wat was that shit wid Jason?

Mark   He's a prick.

Lee   I know he's a prick, he ain't a racist.

Mark   Like you?

Lee   Yeah, gwan, Mark, tell half the story.

Mark   Wass there to tell, yer Lawrie's brother.

Lee   You know I ain't like him.

Mark   Wat you gonna do about Alan King?

Lee   He ain't committed an offence.

Mark   Not yet.

Lee   If he does.

Mark   When.

Lee   I'll have him. So wass this about you quittin the army?

Mark   They didn't like the colour of my eyes.

Lee   Oh come on.

Mark   Don't worry yerself.

Lee   I'm gettin married, next month. Her name's Vicky. She's nice, fit.

Mark   Nice one.

Lee   Come to the wedding. Please.

Lights up in the bar.

Barry   Don't tell me we don't have players who know how to pass, it's like we're scared of the ball or summin.

Lawrie (*aside*)   Them and this 'we'.

Alan   You enjoy supporting our boys then, son?

Barry   They're my boys too.

Lawrie   Armchair supporter.

Barry   I bin to Wembley eight times, I never saw you there.

Alan   Wat was yer first game?

Barry   1990, against Yugoslavia. Mark took me.

Alan   Two–one. Bryan Robson, both goals.

Becks   Put the fuckin ball away! Unreal. They don't get better than that.

Lawrie   Fuck this!

Lee (*approaching*)   Where you going? (*Follows.*)

Lawrie *heads for the pool table. He wipes off the names from the board.*

Lee   You can't do that.

Lawrie (*points at his own face*)   Bothered?

Lee   We still got the second half.

Lawrie   They're gonna walk over us, like everyone else!

Lee   Calm down.

Lawrie   Fuckin taking it! Same old shit like Belgium.

Lee   You give up too easily.

Lawrie   So do they. Why do they always do this to us? I wish I was there, give them Kraut bastards summin to laugh about.

Lee   Enough.

Lawrie   They're got no heart, Lee. We give 'em ours, every single game, and we get fuck all back. If those cunts can't do it on the pitch, we can, we will! We're England!

Lee   Yer a prick.

Lawrie   Yer not playing?

Lee   Fuck off.

Alan (*approaching*)   Set 'em up, Lawrie.

Lee *blocks* **Alan***'s path.*

Alan   Help you, son?

Lee   Leave him alone.

Alan   Spittin image of yer old man.

Lee   Are you deaf?

Alan   Not at all. You and I should have a drink. (*Goes over to* **Lawrie**.) Tragic ennit?

Lawrie   Ninety minutes, Alan, to forget about all the shit out there, and they can't even do that.

Alan   Your dad would be spinning.

They play pool. **Mark** *is at the bar with* **Gina** *who is pouring him a pint.*

Gina   You calm down? Arsehole. You hate Andy Cole.

Mark   I know, I'm sorry. Is Barry behavin himself?

Gina   Rowdy as the rest of them, nuttin I can't handle. He's all right.

Mark   He's stupid. Loves to get led round all the time. The amount of times Mum and Dad had to go to his school, cos of him.

Gina   Like you weren't like that as well.

Mark   He should listen to wat I'm sayin then ennit?

Gina   You and Lee still ain't talkin. I've had blokes fightin over me before, but this is silly.

Mark   I knew you'd dump him.

Gina   He's gettin married.

Mark   He said.

Gina   He's brought her in a few times. Posh bit, really nice. Daddy owns a computer company.

Mark   You coulda called me.

Gina   And get back wid you, yer mad! I hated myself.

Mark   Don't.

Gina   You two were like that. I got between yer.

Mark   Writing was on the wall long before. He listens to his brother too much.

Gina   And yours don't listen at all.

Mark *rejoins the boys.* **Glen** *comes into the pub, he has been beaten up. He is not wearing his jacket. He tries to sneak in without being seen.*

Jimmy   Glenny boy, get yer arse over here, make yourself useful, clear up the glasses from the table.

Glen   I ain't doin nuttin.

Jimmy   You'll do as yer told, I ain't soft like yer bleedin mum. (*Clocks his face.*) Watcha you run into?

Glen   Don't worry yerself.

Jimmy   Gina?

Glen   No.

Jimmy   Over here.

Gina   Jesus! You bin fighting again? Wass the matter wid you? And ware's yer jacket? Ware's yer fuckin jacket?

Glen   Gone ennit.

Gina   Gone where?

Glen   Juss gone.

Gina   Well you better find out ware's it gone, and get it back.

Glen *winces when* **Gina** *grabs his arm.*

Jimmy   Oh Christ, she barely touched yer.

Gina   Glen?

Glen   He took my jacket and my phone ennit? Cos he liked 'em.

Gina   Who?

Glen   Tyrone. Bad T.

Gina   That fuckin little black kid?

Jimmy   You let him take it off yer? You didn't even fight back?

Alan   All right there, Jimmy?

Jimmy   Should be ashamed of yerself.

Alan   Jimmy?

Jimmy   Some fuckin little black kid has had a pop at my boy.

Gina   Little bastard.

Lawrie   Who are they?

Jimmy (*to* **Glen**)   Stop cryin.

Glen   I ain't.

Jimmy   Only got a scratch, stand up straight.

Gina   Dad?

Jimmy   Teach you how to fight, then you can go back, sort 'em out.

Gina   Leave him alone. I'm gonna kill the little cunt.

Mark   You mean black cunt? (*To* **Barry**.) You gettin this?

Gina   Come on, Mark, they were a couple wrong uns you saw 'em yerself, even if I was thinkin it, can you blame me? Wass the matter wid you, look at his face.

Jimmy   A poxy scratch.

Gina   I call it as I see it.

Mark   You all bloody do.

Gina   Would they have nicked his stuff if he was black?

Lawrie   No.

Lee   Ware you goin?

Lawrie   Find this kid.

Lee   Lawrie!

Alan   I'll go.

Lee   You stay. (*Leaves.*)

Becks   You ever seen a more shittier pass than that?

Phil   Come on!

Barry   England!

Jason *comes back with a round of drinks.*

Becks   Wass goin on, Jase?

Jason   Gina's boy got into a fight wid sum black kid.

Phil   As long as he won.

Jason   Only nicked his phone and jacket.

Phil   Little bastard. Sorry, Baz.

Barry   Wat for? (*Screams.*) Come on, you England!

Mark *sits alongside his brother.*

Barry   You still here?

Mark   Juss watchin the game.

Barry   So wat about Dad?

Mark   Karen's lookin after him.

Barry   You don't want to go back home.

Lawrie *and* **Lee** *come in, they have* **Duane**.

Duane   I was comin to give 'em back, right.

Lawrie   Yeah.

Duane   Move, right!

Lawrie   Mouthy little . . .

Duane   Glen, tell 'em man, it weren't me, it was T, right.

Lawrie (*slaps his head*)   You want another?

Mark   Hey, you don't have to hit him.

Lee (*stands between them*)   Let's juss chill, yeah.

Mark   Let the boy go.

Lee   Mark, I swear, I'll arrest yer.

Mark   Me?

Jimmy   Go on, son, game's still playin.

Mark   Fuck the game!

Lee (*to* **Duane**)   Ware's the phone?

Duane *hands it over.*

Duane   I was gonna give it back, I told T, he loves to go too far sometimes, but he don't listen.

Lee   You scared of him?

Duane   Yeah.

Lee   So how come you got the phone and jacket off him?

Duane   I dunno. I juss did.

Lawrie   Lying.

Lee   On yer way.

Duane   Glen, I'm sorry yeah.

Lawrie   He said out!

Duane   Fuck off!

Lawrie *grabs the boy and slings him out.*

Mark   Fuckin . . .

Lawrie   Come on, come on!

Lee   It's over. (*To* **Lawrie**.) Cool it, Lawrie.

Mark   You big it up now ennit?

Jimmy (*to* **Glen**)   See wat trouble you've caused? Wouldn't happen if you stick up for yerself.

Gina   Dad, if you don't stop goin on at him, I'm gonna shove this beer glass into yer face! (*To* **Mark**.) And you, sit down and watch the game.

Alan (*aside*)   Rivers of blood.

Gina   Go upstairs, Glen, clean yer face. Alan, I appreciate your trade, it's always nice to see yer, but I've told you before, I don't want to hear that kind of talk in my pub. Leave that England for whites bollocks outside.

Phil   Fuck's sake!

Jason   Will somebody please score!

Alan   Come on, Jimmy, you know what I'm talking about.

Gina   It's my name above that door.

Alan   I'm sorry, babe, I didn't mean to upset you.

Gina   Then don't say it.

Alan   It's not just me, darling. I've got nothing against the blacks myself, but even you have to admit we've got a problem here. There are too many different races all trying to fit into the same box, how is that supposed to work? Now they've got our kids, talking like them. It's no wonder you feel the same.

Gina   I do not.

Alan   But I just heard you call that kid a black cunt.

Gina   Cos they beat up my son.

Becks   Fuckin chase it!

Alan   Not because he's black? Come on, Gina.

Becks   Chase it!

Alan   It's OK, we are all racists, you know.

Becks   Come on!

Alan   All white people are racists. I heard this black geezer say it once, dead clever. We are racists. We are white, he says. Our history, our culture, our jobs, people on TV, it's all white, if not predominantly. It's not by coincidence, it's by design. Being white is the norm. It always has been. We are the norm. You should have heard him.

Gina   Well, he's wrong.

Alan   Is he?

Jimmy   You were barely on solids when Enoch said his piece, Gina, they were lining to carve him up.

Gina   Good.

Jimmy   They booted him out of his party. All he said was the truth.

Gina   And you agree, you stupid old git.

Jimmy   Look at all the trouble we've got now, it's those fucking black kids from that estate that are causing it all. You know that. I can handle the older blacks, Mark's dad used to drink in here, blindin fella. But these young ones really know how to push it, mouthing off all the time, for no good reason, carryin like the world owes them a favour, bollocks.

The boys watching the match let out a huge sigh.

Jason   That was so close.

Phil   Nice one, Seaman.

Becks   Not bad for an Arsenal man.

Jimmy   Then there's the immigrants.

Gina   Oh Dad.

Jimmy   It's in the papers, you can't deny it, they're everywhere.

Gina   Where, Dad? Where? Down the high street, in here? Where? I don't see 'em.

Lawrie   Tucked away in their nice council homes.

Gina   I'm not hearing this, Lee?

Lee   Leave me out of it.

Lawrie   He knows it's true.

Lee   You a mind-reader?

Lawrie   I'm yer brother.

Jimmy   Papers don't lie, love.

Gina   They lie on a regular basis when it comes to the likes of you. Throw in a pair of tits and they've got you hypnotised. Can you not prove their point please.

Alan   Gina, love, I don't read papers, I haven't picked one up in years. I read books, and I'm tellin you, it's amazing what you read. Pages of it, reams of it, history, telling you, making valid points that the blacks, the non-whites, have absolutely nothing in common with the Anglo-Saxon Celtic culture.

Gina   The what?

Alan   If they want to practise their black culture and heritage, then they should be allowed to do it in their own part of their world. By all means.

Gina   So whites are superior to blacks?

Alan   Yes, if you like.

Gina   Bollocks.

Alan   Consider this, the blacks lived side by side with the Egyptians for thousands of years, only about twenty miles of sand separated them. When the Egyptians came into contact with them, they hadn't even invented the wheel, which the Egyptians had thousands of years ago, they couldn't even copy it.

Gina   Maybe they didn't need it.

Alan   They didn't need the wheel? What has the black man done in the world?

Gina   Thass it! (*Goes back to watching the game.*)

Alan   I'll tell you. When the British and European powers colonised Africa, the colonies had a high standard of civilisation, when the decolonialisation came round, we left these countries economically sound with good administrative government. As soon as the whites left, those blacks are killing each other. Now they've got some of the poorest countries in the world. That's how capable the blacks are of running their own countries and looking after themselves. You look at the rest of the black hemisphere, the Caribbean, rotten with poverty, half of them, now we gave them the means to run their countries efficiently, but we're still pumping aid into these countries to keep them afloat. They can't run themselves; if they can't even live with each other, why should we be expected to live with them as well? We gave them everything they had to carry on, look at us, we won the war militarily, but we lost it in real terms; see the Germans, Japanese, the two strongest economies in the world, because their countries had been so completely destroyed, that money had to be pumped in to rebuild the industries that support these countries. They've managed it, why couldn't the blacks whose countries weren't even destroyed? Why do we always have to keep giving in to their begging bowls? Money which we could do with ourselves, never mind how the poor blacks are suffering around the world.

Lee *gives* **Alan** *a sarcastic, slow hand-clap.*

Alan   You know, Lee, you remind me of this copper I met once, told me this story. This black geezer is parking his car, music blaring out from his speakers. My mate the copper still has to go over and have a word, asks the geezer to turn the music down, neighbours bin complaining. The geezer says no, carrying on like my mate was putting the chains back on him. Anything like that happen to you, Lee?

Lawrie   All the time, par for the course.

Lee   Why don't you tell him my whole life, you seem to know it better than me. (*Goes back to the game.*)

Lawrie (*follows*)   They got no respect, Lee, you know that.

Lee   Yer gonna lecture them about respect, Lawrie?

Jason   We're gonna be 2–0 down.

Becks   We need a goal.

Mark   Doubt it somehow.

Barry   No ideas, not one creative mind.

Jason   Where's Gazza when you need him.

Mark   Gazza of old.

Sharon, **Duane**'s *mum, comes bursting in.*

Sharon   Which one of you bastards hurt my boy?

Jimmy   Gina?

Sharon   Which one of you touch him?

Gina   You wanna calm down please, love.

Sharon   Move!

Gina   Do it, or leave my pub.

Sharon   Yer lucky I don't bring the police, 'bout you rough up my son!

Gina   Yer son nicked my boy's phone.

Sharon   Weren't him.

Gina   He told you that?

Sharon   I said it weren't him. You didn't even give him a chance to explain, you tek one look, see his face, thass it! Hey, don't walk away from me, yer racist bitch!

Gina   Wat did you say?

Sharon   Yer deaf?

Alan   Yer boy was shoutin the odds.

Sharon   You can shut yer mout as well. I bet it was you.

Lee   Calm down, love.

Sharon   Let go of my arm.

Lee   I said calm down.

Sharon   You the police?

Lee   Yes. Now calm yerself down, before I arrest yer.

Sharon   Oi, bitch, I ain't finished wid you. Who did it?

Gina   Get her out of my face.

Lee   Mark, help us out here.

Mark   No.

Sharon   Don't look yer nose down on me right!

Gina   Get out, you silly cow.

Sharon   Come mek me, I'll tear yer fuckin eye out.

Lee   Leave it!

Sharon *strikes out at* **Lee**. **Lawrie** *screams out his brother's name.* **Lee** *restrains her by twisting her arm behind her back.* **Sharon** *shrieks in pain.*

Lawrie   You awright, son?

Lee   Yes!

Lawrie   Are you sure?

Mark   Lee!

Lee   You had yer chance, back off.

Phil   Wass goin on?

Becks (*sees the commotion*)   Jesus! Yer brother, Baz.

Barry   So wat?

Mark   Lee, get off her, man.

Lee   I told you, Mark.

Sharon   Bitch!

Lee   Jimmy, call the police.

Act Two

Same location as Act One.

Jason, **Barry**, **Becks** *are watching the game. It is a few minutes into the second half.* **Phil** *is watching the commotion going on outside the window.*

Barry I'd give Posh Spice a fucking good seeing to I would. Fuck her till she screams. I'd strip off all her clothes, her damp and sticky knickers, I'd lay her down on the floor, frig her pussy with my fingers, rubbing away at her clit, till she had an orgasm. Then I'd give her a fuck, long lingering fuck. And she'll take it cos she's juicy and sexed up. I'll find out if she takes it up the arse. I'll do it. You hear me, Beckham? Thass wat I'm gonna do to yer fucking wife, if you don't score some goals!

Jason Easy, Barry.

Barry He's gettin on my nerves.

Becks Ain't he carryin sum injury?

Phil His left knee, I think.

Becks I bet he's thinkin about Man U. They got a Champions League game soon, he don't want to get injured. Playing for England don't mean nuttin to them any more.

Barry Three lions on the shirt.

Becks You'd rather see Man U lose, and England win?

Barry We ain't watchin Man U, we're watchin England; when England play, Man U don't exist. Bloody money they're on.

Phil More police out there, they're tellin that Sharon to shut it.

Jason Wat still? Just cart her off, the mad bitch.

Phil She's got sum mouth.

Barry (*chants*)   ENGLAND! ENGLAND!

Phil Now Mark's gettin stuck in, he's gonna get nicked an all, if he ain't careful.

Barry   Come on!

Phil   Now she's mouthin off at Mark.

Jason   Gina?

Phil   Sharon! Tellin him she don't need his help. Barry, shouldn't you be out there?

Barry   ENGLAND!

Phil   Baz!

Barry   Wat?

Phil   He's your brother, you should be backing him up.

Barry   I'm watchin the game.

Becks   You ain't gonna miss anything.

Barry   So why are you still here then?

Jason   Cos we follow England.

Barry   Wat you tryin to say, Jase?

Jason   Nuttin.

Barry   I'm not white enuff for England?

Jason   Oh behave yerself.

Barry   Is it?

Jason   You lot need to chill out.

Barry   Black people.

Jason   Awright, yeah! Black people. Going off on one all the time. Whenever someone says the slightest thing. All yer doing is pissing people off.

Barry   All I'm doing is watching the match.

Jason   So watch it! 'kin 'ell.

Becks   Awright, boys, come on, let's bring out the peace pipe. Look, Kieron Dyer's on, he might do summin. (*Goes behind the bar.*) Who wants a drink, Phil? Come on, free round.

Phil   Awright quick, top this up.

Barry   Sharon is nuttin but a mouthy cow. She wants to get nicked, thass her problem.

Becks   Yes, Baz, watever, mate, calm yerself.

Barry   I am calm.

Becks   Good.

Barry (*chants*)   ENGLAND!

Jimmy *and* **Glen** *come back in.*

Gina   Crazy bitch.

Jimmy   Awright, love.

Gina   She's a fuckin loon. (*To* **Jason** *and* **Barry**.) Get yer bloody feet off my seats.

Jimmy (*to* **Becks**)   Settling in? Get yer arse out of there. Yer a thievin bastard, Julian, juss like yer old man.

Becks   I was gonna pay.

Jimmy   Too right you'll pay, how much you had, you little . . . ?

Jason   He ain't had much, Jimmy, I swear, come on, whose round, Phil?

Phil   Na.

Jason   Yer as tight-arsed as Becks, you.

Barry   I'll get 'em in.

Jason   You got the lass one.

Barry   I don't mind.

Becks   Yeah, Jase, shut up, same again please, Barry my man.

Phil   And me.

Barry *goes to the bar.*

Gina   Sorry for wat I said. That Sharon juss wound me up. You know me, I ain't got a problem with nobody.

Barry   It's awright.

Gina   Yer brother won't see it that way.

Barry   I ain't my brother.

Gina   OK.

Barry   I ain't losin my rag awright.

Gina   OK.

Barry   Stop sayin OK. I'm juss sayin, I'm tellin yer, I'm not my brother. I want to watch the match, wat Mark does is up to him. I don't want to be like 'em. Go all mad all the time, like we've all got an attitude. I don't.

Lee *comes in followed by* **Lawrie** *and* **Alan**.

Lawrie   You soft cunt. I'm talkin to you.

Becks   Wat?

Lawrie   He only tells his mates to let that Sharon off.

Lee   I didn't see the point in taking it through.

Alan   The point was made when they put the cuffs on her.

Lawrie   She only bit one of them.

Alan   You can't change people like that.

Lee   And you juss had to stand there, stirring it.

Lawrie   Lee, she went for yer, she coulda had a knife.

Lee   You see knives everywhere, Lawrie. Whenever we go out, whenever you see a black person, you think they've got a knife.

Lawrie   Well, pardon me for caring.

Lee   I'm awright.

Lawrie   Ungrateful or wat eh? Don't come crying to me when one of them stabs yer again.

Alan   You want to be a bit more grateful, son.

Lee   Get out of my face.

Alan   Comfortable, is it? The fence you're sitting on? Wake up.

Lawrie   Oh leave him. I don't know wass the matter wid him.

Alan   Don't ever lose your rag like that again.

Lawrie   Eh?

Alan   You were this much from getting arrested as well. It seems par for the course with you. Is it any wonder no one listens to us?

Lawrie   Hold up.

Alan   I couldn't believe my eyes when I saw you lot running amok in Belgium this summer. Fighting in the streets, smashing up bars and caffs. What was that?

Lawrie   It's about been English. All the things you've said.

Alan   That wasn't been English, you were acting like a bunch of savages. You were no better than the coons.

Lawrie   It's how I feel.

Alan   That's no excuse.

Lawrie   There's nuttin that makes me wanna say I'm proud to be English.

Alan   No one wants to speak up for you. It's not fashionable.

Lawrie   Right.

Alan   But they want to speak up for the blacks, queers, Pakis, that's fashionable.

Lawrie   Yes!

Alan   You just want to run out and beat the shit out of someone. I understand.

Lawrie   So wass the problem?

Alan   It scares people off.

Lawrie   It don't scare me.

Alan   You don't speak for the country.

Lawrie   So, what?

Alan   It's smart-arses who are in control of this country, on every level, and we have to be as clever. Keep this country white, away from the blacks. They're just marginalising them. Don't let them marginalise us. Gina's right, get your head out of crap like the *Sun*, get down the library, read a book, read ten books.

Lawrie   I hate books.

Alan   Not any more. I'll give you a list. Because knowledge is power. You want to hide something from the black man, put it in a book.

Lawrie   I'd rather kill 'em.

Alan   Read.

They continue their game of pool. **Lee** *is by the bar with* **Gina**. *The lads are still watching the game.*

Jason   We should be wearing our home kit. The blue and white.

Becks   Why?

Jason   We always seem to play worse in our red. Wat do you think?

Phil   I think yer talkin shit.

Jason   Look.

Phil   We wore red in '66, and won.

Becks   We wore white and blue in the semis in Italy and lost.

Barry   We wore all white against the Argies in '98 and lost.

Phil   And in Euro '96, against the fuckin Germans again!

Barry   No we didn't.

Phil   We did lose.

Barry   I mean, we wore all blue for that, yer muppet.

Phil   Oh right. I musta bin thinkin about the other game.

Jason   I hated that blue kit.

Becks   Everyone hated it.

Barry   Our home kit then was all right, I like that. I don't know why they changed it. I really liked the touch of light blue it had, on the collars and cuff, and that bit on the shorts.

Boys (*agreeing*)   Yeah.

Barry   Nice.

Phil   I thought the last one we had was awright as well, with the blue and the red stripes down the sides. With a touch of white on the blue shorts.

Boys (*agreeing*)   Yeah.

Phil   Very nice.

Gina   I don't care what colour she is. She deserves to be carted off. Mouthin off like that.

Lee   Lawrie didn't help. I'm so sick of this. He won't listen.

Gina   He loves his football.

Lee   From the day he was born. Thirtieth July, 1966.

Gina   And?

Lee   Day England won the World Cup.

Gina   Shut up.

Lee   On my life.

Gina   No way!

Lee   Dad wanted to name him after Geoff Hurst. (**Gina** *laughs.*) Mum wouldn't have it. You know how many times I've heard Dad going on about that match, describing every goal? When England ruled the world again for four glorious years, when Enoch, best prime minister we never had, spoke the truth. Lawrie loved that shit.

Gina   Wait till I tell Dad.

Lee   I can't do it, Gina.

Gina   Do wat?

Lee   The job. He's my brother, he gets on my tits, but I feel like agreeing with him sometimes. Cos thass the bitta Dad rubbing off on me. But that's not the kind of copper I want to be. But then I'm thinkin it's too late. Whenever a black geezer comes up to me now, I'm shakin. I'm angry. All I wanted to do that night, Gina, was calm it all down. All the things they moan about on the telly, all the things police officers don't do, that they hate, what they should be doing, well, I was doing it! All of it! I was treating all those people at that rave like people, not black people, but people! I wanted to understand, I was trying to listen, I wanted to prove that not all coppers are the same.

Gina Lee?

Lee Then he stabbed me. That fuckin black bastard stabbed me. I ain't racist, Gina, but it's how I felt, it's how I still feel, is that so wrong? That bloke tried to kill me, and he got away with it.

Gina I ain't judging yer.

Lee All I wanted to do was help.

Gina There's yer problem. Don't help them. Don't try to understand them. Do yer job. Don't lose yerself in anger, Lee.

Phil Oh come on!

Jason Fuck's sake

Becks They're gettin comfortable again, we gotta keep possession, gotta push 'em back, see how they like it in their own half for once.

Jason Oh yu useless wankers, come on. Please! I'm beggin yer!

The boys get excited as Le Saux makes a run.

Yes, yes!

Phil Come on, Le Saux!

Becks Come on, Le Saux!

Jason Fuckin cross it!

German defender heads it away.

Phil Shit.

Jason Wass he head that away for? Let us have one, yer greedy cunts!

Barry *leaves his seat.*

Jason   Ware you goin, Baz? Baz? (*Mimics* **Barry**.) All I'm doing is watchin the watch.

Barry *goes to the pool table.*

Barry   My name was on the board.

Alan   Was it?

Barry   I was supposed to be playing next.

Lawrie   Yeah?

Alan   Lawrie?

Lawrie *steps aside as* **Barry** *picks up a cue.*

Alan   We are all friends here.

Barry *and* **Alan** *play pool together.* **Lawrie** *watches on.*

Alan   So, how is it going?

Barry   Awright.

Alan   That was a splendid couple of goals you got this morning. Did you ever think about turning pro?

Barry   Had a trial for Fulham. Didn't cut it.

Alan   Their loss. Who do you follow?

Barry   Man U.

Alan   Man U?

Barry   Ain't they good enough?

Alan   Comedian.

Lawrie   I'd shit on Man U.

Alan   Yes, that is very nice, Lawrie, but no one is asking you, are they? (*To* **Barry**.) Follow your local team, what is the matter with you? It's about loyalty. Family even. You don't choose your family, they are just there, from the moment you are born. Through thick and thin. They're with you, you're with them. You are born in the town of

your team. They are your family as well, your blood. And
every Saturday, you are watching them play, willing them
on to score, then another, and another. Final whistle goes.
And you all roar and cheer. You can't wait till next
Saturday. Starts all over again. And no matter where you
go, where you move. You take them with you, in your heart.
When was the last time you've been to Old Trafford?

Barry   Does it matter? I follow them.

Alan   But do you feel them?

Barry   Course.

Alan   Where were you born?

Barry   Shepherds Bush.

Alan   Queens Park Rangers.

Barry   They're shit.

Alan   They're yer blood.

Barry   I ain't following them.

Alan   Just as you like.

Barry   So who do you follow?

Alan   Aston Villa. What are you laughing at? My dad
followed Villa. I was born in Birmingham. We all moved to
London when I was ten. But I took them with me, in my
heart.

Barry   You still watch them?

Alan   Whenever I can. I can still remember my first game.
My dad took me when I was nine. 1961 it was. We beat
Sheffield Wednesday 4–1. We played them off the Park.
And it was John Dixon's last game for Villa.

Barry   Who?

Alan   One of the best players we ever had. He stayed with
the club for seventeen years. He could score goals as well as

make them and play all five forward positions as well as his own, left half. He was our captain when we won the cup in '57. What a game. I've still got the programme. Still, Man U, are a blinding side, can't argue with that. Your Andy Cole is doing all right for himself, and the other one, wasshisface.

Barry   Dwight Yorke. Used to be one of yours.

Alan   Yes all right, don't rub it in. Class player he was.

Barry   Still is.

Alan   Always smiling. Should have seen the verbal he got from some of the fans though when he came back to Villa, wearing a Man U shirt. Black this, black that! I have never heard anything like it. What was it that them Liverpool fans used to chant at John Barnes when he first started playing for them? Lawrie?

Lawrie   Better dead, than a nigger in red.

Alan   Right. Must be hard for you as well.

Barry   I never get it.

Alan   Well, then you are lucky. Isn't he lucky, Lawrie?

Lawrie   Yeah, he's lucky.

Alan   It's good to hear that. It gives hope to us all. You are a black person who everyone sees as a person first, not their colour.

Barry   I am a person.

Alan   That is what I said. Never mind the ones who only see you as a black person. Have you ever run into those people, son?

Barry   No.

Alan   The ones who think being white is the norm?

Barry   I said no.

Alan   Awright, son. I'm just trying to put myself in your shoes. No need to get jumpy.

Barry   I'm not jumpy.

Alan   I understand where you are coming from, I really do. You're from this country, you live here, born here, but there are still a few, the minority, that won't accept you.

Barry   I am accepted.

Alan   Course you are. I mean, you're not like the Asians, are you?

Barry   Damn right I ain't.

Alan   No. I don't see your lot owning hundreds of shops all lined up next to each other down Southall. Cutting yourselves off from the rest of the country. Not speaking the Queen's English. Your lot ain't like that at all. You're sweet with us now. Two shots. It must get to you though, when you meet the ones who just want to know about the black experience.

Barry .   That ain't me.

Alan   White girls, eyeing you up all the time, because they're curious, about the myth. White guys wanting to be your mates, because they are curious as well. Penis envy, hardly acceptance, is it, Barry?

Barry   Wass the matter wid yer?

Alan   Right-on liberals, stupid lefties, all lining up, wanting to do you all a favour, they're just scared you'll lose yer tempers, mug them after work, how equal is that? All that talk, understanding, deep down they know, they believe, blacks are inferior, whites are superior. You must feel really small when you meet people like that . . .

Barry   . . . Look, juss fuck off, awright!

Barry *rejoins the others.*

Alan   Barry? Barry son?

Lawrie　Wat was that?

Alan　Reeling them in, throwing them back. The boy's got no idea who his friends are.

Phil　Oh look, he's bringin a sub on.

Becks　Oh nice one, Keegan, yer muppet!

Barry (*screams*)　Come on, you England!

Jason　Baz?

Barry　Stand up, if you won the war! Stand up, if you won the war!

Jason　Not again.

Barry　You dirty German bastard! You dirty German bastard!

Jason　Barry!

Barry　ENGLAND!

Jimmy　Oi, Lionel Ritchie, keep it down yeah.

Mark *comes back into the pub.*

Jimmy　You going to be nice now?

Mark　Leave me alone, Jimmy.

Jimmy　I can't do that. Leave the attitude outside, Mark.

Mark　I'm juss watching the game.

Jimmy　Wat happened to that happy little smilin coloured kid I used to know eh? Good little boy? Go on, sit down.

Mark *joins the boys, he sits near* **Lee.**

Jason　Wat do you call that?

Lee　You go to the station?

Mark　They had to drag her in there.

Lee　She was resisting arrest, Mark.

Mark   Like an animal.

Lee   Wat were they supposed to do?

Mark   Four coppers, one woman.

Lee   You saw how she was.

Mark   Four coppers, one woman.

Lee   You never listen, it's your point of view or nuttin.

Jimmy   Mark?

Lee   We're all right, Jimmy. (*To* **Mark**.) I tried to calm the situation as well as I could.

Mark   You takin the piss?

Lee *goes to the bar.*

Mark   Wat you runnin for?

Lee   Top it up, Gina.

Mark   Wat you runnin for?

Gina   Leave it out, Mark.

Mark   You really think she deserved to be treated like that?

Lee   Why you always pushin me?

Mark   Do yer, Lee?

Gina   He was doing his job.

Mark   Stick together, like old times ennit?

Gina   Oh piss off!

Lee   Bloody . . .

Mark   Say it, Lee, call me a nigger again.

Lee   He really wants me to.

Mark   It's wat I am!

Gina   Will you stop.

Mark   You didn't want me havin her cos I was black.

Gina   Oh Mark.

Lee   White guy steals white girl from black guy, it juss doesn't happen, does it, Mark? It's the other way round.

Mark   You wanted to finish wid me cos I was black.

Gina   I finished wid you cos you were boring. You were boring in bed, and you were boring to talk to. If you woke up tomorrow as white as I am, you'll still be boring.

Jimmy (*approaching*)   I warned you, son, come on.

Gina   Leave it alone, Dad.

Barry   ENGERLAND! ENGERLAND! ENGERLAND!

Becks   Awright, Baz, Jesus!

Gina   Will you sort him out please.

Mark (*approaching*)   Barry, come on.

Barry   Wass up, bro? My brother! He's more English than any of you, he's protected this country. He's protected you! Come on, you England! Stand up if you won the war!

Gina   Take him home.

Barry   Game ain't finished.

Mark   He'll be awright. Come on!

Becks   Wat again? They tugging each other's plonkers or wat?

Lights on **Barry** *and* **Mark** *in the Gents.*

Barry   Fucking bastard! 'bout I ain't English.

Mark   Who?

Barry   That geezer Alan. Talkin to me like I'm stupid.

Mark   You shoulda stayed away from him.

Barry   Shoulda told him about Euro '96. Wembley, Holland, the game!

Mark   I know.

Barry   We killed them, oh man, we killed them! Four goals, class written all over them. The best match since '66. Saw it wid me own eyes. You, me and Lee. Cheering the lads on, singing our hearts out. I backed you and Lee up when those bunch of Dutch fans tried to have a pop, we kicked every bit of shit out of them. Then we roared, right into their faces, England! Shoulda told him that, then give him a fuckin slap.

Mark   See? They only pretend to be yer friends.

Barry   I don't have problems with the rest of them.

Mark   Not yet.

Barry   What are we, a couple of Pakis now? Wass happened to you?

Mark   I juss saw Sharon dragged by her hair.

Barry   So what, she's a loudmouth bitch. You told me yerself, thass why you dumped her.

Mark   So, she deserve that?

Barry   Stop using her as an excuse.

Mark   I ain't.

Barry   You are.

Mark   Look, yer right, I don't want to go home either. I don't want to see Dad like that. So let's get out of here, check out Daryl and dem, I bet they're watchin the match.

Barry   I don't like Daryl and his mates.

Mark   You shouldn't be afraid of yer own people.

Barry   I ain't afraid of them, I juss don't like some of 'em. I don't fit in. You feel the same, Mark, well, used to. I loved

the way you were with them. Them carryin on with their
bad attitude, you used to slap them down, they were havin a
laugh. Wass the army done to you? (*Takes off his shirt, shows
his tattoo.*) Look.

Mark   Barry . . .

Barry   Thass British, thass us! Don't laugh at me, it's us.
Show me yours.

Mark   Get off.

Barry   You were gonna wear it wid pride, you said. You
didn't care who sees your red, white and blue, or who
laughs, cos you ain't ending up like some black cunt. We are
British, we are here! We kick arse with the best of them.
God save the Queen, you told me that.

Mark   They don't want us here, Barry.

Barry   We were born here.

Mark   They don't care.

Lights up on the bar.

Glen *comes down. The screen turns blue again. Lads groan.*

Becks   Oh shut up, yer gettin on my tits now, the lot of
yer.

Gina   How's my little prince then?

Glen   Awright.

Gina   Yer still gorgeous. (*Kisses him on the cheek.*)

Glen (*embarrassed*)   Mum?

Jimmy   You stopped cryin then?

Gina   Dad?

She holds up a beer glass to remind her father of her earlier threat.

I thought you were going to watch telly?

Glen   Nuttin's on.

Gina   Watch a video then. (*Gets a fiver from the till.*) Here, go down the video shop.

Glen   I don't want to go out.

Gina   You can't stay in here for ever, sweetheart. Sooner or later you're going to have to face those boys 'gain.

Glen   I know I have to face them again, Mum, but I don't want to do it now.

Gina   Calm down, I'm on your side, darlin. Go on, sit with the lads, watch the game. Go on, they don't bite.

Glen *joins* **Lee** *and the others. They all greet him warmly.*

Jason   Awright, Glen?

Phil   How you doing, son?

Lawrie   You want a Coke, Glen?

Glen   Yeah.

Gina   Yeah wat?

Glen   Yeah please.

Gina   Cheers, Lawrie.

Lawrie   Top this up as well, Gina.

Jason   Come on, Glen, cheer up.

Becks   Wat goes around, comes around, those black kids will get theirs.

Phil   This whole area is going down.

Becks   See, Glen, wat you have to do, is get a little gang of yer own, you and a few white lads.

Jason   Don't let Gina hear yer.

Lee   Or me!

Becks   There's nuttin wrong wid that?

Lee   You sure?

Becks   I've seen black gangs, Asian gangs, how can it be racist, if them boys are doing it? Get yerself some white boys, Glen, stick together, show sum pride. (*To screen.*) Unlike these wankers!

Lee (*to* **Glen**)   Oi, you ignore every word he said, you hear me?

Phil   Glen, come here, got a joke for yer. There's this black geezer right, Winston, nice fella, well thick. Anyway he's feelin a sick one morning, so he rings up his boss at work sayin (*puts on worst West Indian accent*), Ey, boss, I not come work today, I really sick. I got headache, stomach ache, and my legs hurt, I not come work. The boss goes, Oh Winston, you know I really need you today. It's important. Now, when I feel like this, I go to my wife, and tell her to give me sex. That makes me feel better and I can go to work. You should try that. Two hours later, Winston calls back, saying, Boss, boss, I did wat you said and I feel great, man! I be back at work real soon, boss. By the way, you got a nice house!

The boys roar with laughter.

Oops, I can see a smile, a smile is coming, he's smiling, he's smiling!

Boys cheer.

Lee   Is anyone watchin the match here?

Phil   What match?

Jason   Useless cunts.

Phil   Ere, Glen, come here. Yer mum still got that same boyfriend?

Glen   No. Why?

Phil   Nuttin.

Barry *and* **Mark** *come back.*

Becks   Barry my man, were you bin?

Jason   Have a nice tug, did yer? (*Rubs* **Barry***'s head.*)

Barry   Don't.

Jason   Oooh, handbag.

Gina   We happy over there?

Mark   Sweet as, Gina.

Alan   Fancy a game, son?

Mark   I'm outta here.

Alan   Come on, one game.

Mark   Play me like you did my brother?

Alan   I have no idea what you mean.

Mark   Don't even bother.

Alan   All right then, I won't. But I bet you've fantasised about having a debate with someone like me. You want to shoot me down, find flaws in my twisted logic.

Mark   I've fantasised about kicking the shit out of someone like you.

Alan   That would be too easy. You and I agree on similar things.

Mark   Move.

Alan   (*quotes*)   'They don't want us here, Barry.' I was in one of the cubicles. I overheard.

Mark   We got nuttin in common.

Alan   Let's see. (*Offers a cue-stick.*) Do you know what the main thing is that I hear people moan about? It's that, they don't think they can talk about it. They can't voice their concerns, how they feel, they're too scared to be called racists by the PC brigade. Now, I don't know about you, Mark, but I think we've got to get through that, because if people can't talk to each other, different communities, being honest, we are not going to get anywhere. So, come on. You and me, let's pave the way. If you want to stop people from being like me, then you had better start listening to people like me.

Mark *takes the cue-stick.*

Alan   So, army boy . . .

Mark   Ex.

Alan   What happened?

Mark   My CO was a racist wanker, so I smacked him one.

Alan   Nasty.

Mark   For him.

Alan   Do you know what you are going to do now?

Mark   You gonna give me a job? Let's get on with it.

Alan   Putting me straight. I like that. Do you watch TV, Mark?

Mark (*sarcastic*)   Once or twice.

Alan   All of those chat shows they have in the morning. *Trisha*, *Kilroy*, Richard & Judy.

Mark   Is there a point coming?

Alan   Any time they have some big issue to bang on about, they invite the general public, the great working class to have their say. Live debates, phone-ins, big mistake. I shudder when I hear them speak. Cringe. They are so inarticulate, they cannot string two sentences together. They are on live TV, and I'm screaming at the telly, articulate, you stupid sap. And their arguments, their points of view, Jesus Christ! So ignorant, stupid, dumb, deeply flawed, simplistic. It's obvious they have never read a book in their lives. I've seen black people on those programmes as well, son, and no offence, but it seems as though they've been eating retard sandwiches. Have you ever felt that way about them?

Mark   No.

Alan   Come on, Mark, honesty. Play the game.

Mark   Yes.

Alan   You hate the way they talk.

Mark   Yes.

Alan   You want to scream at them, they're letting the side down.

Mark   Yes.

Alan   Make your point, and make it well.

Mark   You gonna make yours?

Alan   Like me, you want to be better than that, but, unlike me, you know, wisely I might add, that can never happen. Not here.

Mark   Wat?

Alan   Look at us, Mark. (*Points at everyone.*) The white working class. You think it was an accident we are all as thick as shit? It's because of the powers that be. I know their game. Britain needs people like Lawrie to do the shit jobs. It can't have everyone bein a doctor or a lawyer, the economy would fall apart. Give them the shit life, shit education, the works. And do you know who we are going to blame for not getting ahead? You. Why? Because you're different, because it's convenient, because it's easier to blame you than it is to think about what's really going on, and the reason why we don't think is because we can't, and the reason we can't is the Hoo-ra-Henrys made sure of it. Spin us a tale, put it in the tabloids, we'll buy it. We'll blame anyone thass different for our own shortcomings. They want us to fight, they want us to fight you. We'll fight, but not the way they think. This is our country, we made it, and we don't belong in the gutter, because they say we do.

Mark   But we do, yeah?

Alan   You're not dragging us down.

Mark   Gimme one good reason why I shouldn't wrap this cue-stick round yer head.

Alan   Because I can help you.

Mark   By sending me back to ware I come from?

Alan   Eventually.

Mark   Convincing all my brothers and sisters to do the same, work for you?

Alan   It's not as uncommon as you think. Some of our European friends have had black and Jewish branches. We're thinking of setting up our own ethnic liaison committee.

Mark   Yer certifiable.

Alan   Don't tell me you're happy wid the way yer lot carry on, especially round here. They can't fall out of bed without getting into trouble.

Mark   I know how I feel, and yeah they make me sick to be black. All they're doin is provin you and me right. But I don't want to be right, any more, I want to be proved wrong. I'm sick of being angry.

Alan   That's soppy talk.

Mark   I want to be who I want.

Alan   You are telling me you want to spend the rest of your life walking round like an arsehole with your cap in hand, waiting for the great white man to save you? He wants to kill you. Have some respect for yourself, stand up on your own two feet, make your own mark in the world, no one else will do it for you.

Mark (*laughs*)   You sound like my old man.

Alan   Wise man, was he?

Mark   He thought he was.

Alan   What did he do?

Mark   Bus conductor.

Alan   How long?

Mark   Thirty-odd years.

Alan   And I bet he had to scrimp and save all his life.

Mark   Who doesn't?

Alan   But that is not what he wanted when he came here, I bet. Or are you telling me he left the sun and sea of the West Indies for the grey skies of London to be a bus conductor? The poor sod probably wanted to party all night, sleep with as many white women as possible, and smoke loads of shit.

Mark *bursts out laughing.*

Alan   You looked at him, and you thought, no way am I ending up like that. But you are, it's still happening. That is why you should go. Tell this country what to go and do with itself. No one is going to help you.

Mark   I don't want help.

Alan   You all want it, you're lost without us.

Mark   I want a chance.

Alan   But it us white people that's pulling all the strings, Mark. We'll decide how many chances you get. We're never going to change, so stop wishing. Show me one white person who has ever treated you as an equal, and I will show you a liar. The minute one of them says they are going to treat you as an equal, they're not. Because, in order to do that, they have to see you differently. It will never come as naturally as when they see another white person. All this multiculturalism. Eating a mango once a year at the Notting Hill Carnival is still a long way from letting your kids go to a school that is overrun with Pakis and blacks.

Mark   Wat is it wid you?

Alan   We come from different parts of the world, son, we have different ways of living.

Mark   I'm English.

Alan   No you're not.

Mark   I served in Northern Ireland. I swore an oath of allegiance to the flag.

Alan   Oh please.

Mark   How English are you? Where do you draw the line as to who's English. I was born in this country. And my brother. You're white, your culture comes from northern Europe, Scandinavia, Denmark. Your people moved from there thousands of years ago, long before the Celtic people and the Beeker people, what? You think cos I'm black, I don't read books. Where do you draw the line?

Alan   That's exactly the kind of ridiculous question we have to deal with.

Mark   Answer me.

Alan   The fact is, Mark, that the white British are a majority racial group in this country, therefore it belongs to the white British. If that was the case, what you're asking, we'd all be putting ourselves back into the sea. Because that is where we all originally came from, isn't it?

Mark   Yer full of shit.

Alan   We say that the people of European, white European descent are entitled to settle in Britain. Or the rest of Europe, where they are. We regard our racial cousins, the Americans, Canadians, as British. They've been implanted there over the centuries, now why should we take a time on it? The fact is the majority of blacks haven't been in this country for centuries, a few yes, maybe, but that's it. You've been here, predominantly, in your own numbers, three generations at most. That gives you squatters' rights. We're taking those squatters' rights away from you. You have given nothing to Britain, and you have never served any purpose in British history.

Mark   Oh, so the fact that thousands of black soldiers died during the war is lost on you.

Alan   Not as many as the Brits.

Mark   Or the fact that in the eighteenth century, there was a thriving black community, living right here?

Alan   Not as many as the Brits.

Mark   With their own pubs, churches, meeting places. Or the fact that in 1596, there were so many black slaves over here, working for their white owners, putting money in their pockets, doing all the work, that Queen Elizabeth saw them as a threat and wanted them out.

Alan   What are you on?

Mark   How many black Roman soldiers were here, when they came over and built your roads?

Alan   You're losing it.

Mark   Were you bullied at school, Alan? Couple of black kids nicked your dinner money? Or did your wife run off with a big black man? And I mean big black man? Or was it your mum?

Alan   If you're so smart, son, how come you still haven't caught up with us?

Mark   Cos you love pushing us down.

Alan   Well, push us back. You've had thousands of years. What are you waiting for, you useless bastards. Always some excuse. Can't you people take account for what you are doing to yourselves, instead of blaming us every five seconds?

Mark   You are to blame.

Alan   If you cannot hold your own to account for what they are doing, then we will be left to take drastic measures.

Mark   Is that right?

Alan   Lack of accountability creates anger, Mark, look at all the hate in the world, and it will twist some people's logic, just like Lawrie's, and flavour thought. Bad things are motivated purely by anger. You lot need to feel we will be held to account for what we've done, well, we need to feel it from you first.

Mark   You don't have the right.

Alan   Why's that?

Mark   Because yer white.

Alan   Who's the bigot now?

Mark   Go fuck yourself.

Alan   Face it, son, you're nothing but a ticked box. You will never be equal to us, and you know it.

Mark   You won't win. Thass wat I know.

Alan   We already have.

Mark (*chants*)   We shall not, we shall not be moved!

Alan   Mark?

Mark   We shall not, we shall not be moved, we shall not, we shall not be moved, we shall not, we shall not be moved, we shall not, we shall not be moved, we shall not, we shall not be moved, we shall not, we shall not be moved, we shall not, we shall not be moved, Baz!

Barry (*joins in*)   We shall not, we shall not be moved! We shall not, we shall not be moved –

Mark/Barry   We shall not, we shall not be moved! We shall not, we shall not be moved, And we'll go on, to win the great world cup, we shall not be moved!

Phil   You two pissed?

Barry/Mark   ENGLAND! (*Clap.*) ENGLAND! (*Clap.*)
ENGLAND! (*Clap.*) ENGLAND! (*Clap.*) ENGLAND!

Lawrie (*approaching*)   You awright, Alan?

Alan   They can't even see when someone is doing them a
favour. I've got a good mind to set you on him.

Lawrie   Why don't yer?

Alan   Don't be stupid.

Lawrie   I'll be careful.

Lee *comes out of the Gents.*

Lawrie   No fall-back on you. Say the word and he's dead.

Lee   Who's dead?

Alan   We are.

Lee   Who's dead, Lawrie?

Lawrie   No one.

Lee (*to* **Alan**)   You, fuck off.

Alan   Excuse me?

Lee   I'm talking to my brother.

Alan (*approaching*)   Another Scotch, Gina.

Lawrie   Take a shot.

Lee *throws the cue-stick across the table.*

Lawrie   Oh thass clever, Jimmy will love you if you break
his cue.

Lee   You touch Mark, I'll have yer.

Lawrie   Easy, tiger.

Lee   I've had enuff of yer shit, Lawrie.

Lawrie   Oh why are you still sticking up for them?

Lee   It weren't Mark that stabbed me.

Lawrie   They're scum.

Lee   I won't let you.

Lawrie   Who looked after yer, held yer hand every night while you had yer nightmares, Lee? Do you still see him when you shut yer eyes? That coon coming at yer with his knife?

Lee   It's me he tried to kill.

Lawrie   And I want to kill every one of them.

Lee   Yer never happy unless yer gettin stuck in on someone's head.

Lawrie   Go on, fuck off. Go back to yer posh bird.

Lee   If you weren't such a prick, you'd come live with us.

Lawrie   I ain't no ponce.

Lee   You need looking after.

Lawrie   Yer my kid brother, you don't look after me. God, I feel like I want to explode sometimes.

Lee   See.

Lawrie   I woulda killed someone by now if it weren't for Alan. I really would. I can feel myself wantin to do it sometimes. Every morning when I wake up. I wanna make a bomb or summin, go down Brixton and blow every one of them up.

Lee (*slaps his face*)   I'll kill you first. Do you want me to choose, Lawrie?

Lawrie   Do wat you want.

Lee   I want me brother.

Lawrie   I'm here.

Lee   Ask Alan about Reading, watch his face drop.

Lawrie Wat about it?

Lee Him and his lot were recruiting teenagers. One of them got a little excited, beat up some Asian kid. Alan, blindin geezer, didn't even wait for the Old Bill to breathe down his neck. He gave up that boy's name so fast, well desperate to save his arse. My new DS comes from Reading. He worked on the case. You want that to be you?

Lawrie That kid was stupid, he got caught.

Lee Why won't you ever listen to me?

Lawrie I ain't you, Lee.

Lee Fucking Dad.

Lawrie (*snaps*) Leave it!

Lee Don't think I won't warn him.

Lawrie You think thass gonna stop me?

The final whistle blows. The game is finished.

Jason Wat a load of fuckin bollocks.

Screen shows Kevin Keegan walking away with his head down. Sound of the crowd booing.

Yeah, nice one, lads, boo the cunt!

The boys join in the jeering.

Jimmy Southgate in midfield!

Phil Cole up front wid Owen!

Becks Lass game at Wembley!

Phil You see that? Hamman's wearing an England sweater.

Barry Who swapped jerseys?

Phil It's a number 4 he's wearin.

Becks Southgate.

Barry   Fuckin Kraut lover. We lose 1–0 and he's given him his jersey.

Becks's *phone rings.*

Becks (*answers*)   Awright, Rob? Yeah I know, fuckin disgrace ennit? Wat? Rob goes the fans are booing Keegan.

Jason   They wanna fuckin lynch him.

Mark   Come on, who's drinkin?

Phil   Yeah, go on then, with any luck, I might drown the memory of this day away.

Barry   Lass game at Wembley.

Mark   They're buildin a new one.

Barry   Won't be the same.

Becks   Awright, see yer in a bit. (*Hangs up.*) Rob's gonna come over. Well, come on, let's have some beer.

Jason   Yeah whose round is it, Becks?

Mark   Na yer awright, I'll get 'em in.

Becks   Cheers, Mark.

Mark   Barry?

Barry *goes with his brother.*

Jason   You are so bleeding tight, Becks. You ain't put yer hand in yer pocket all day, have yer?

Becks   Is it my fault our coloured friends over there are so generous? Come on, smile, yer cunts. We can still get to the finals, it's not impossible. We'll beat the Germans next year.

Phil   Oh yeah, we're really gonna hammer them on their own turf, ain't we?

Jason   Wat do you reckon the score will be, Becks, 5–1 to us?

Becks   Sod yer then.

Lee *approaches* **Barry** *and* **Mark**.

Lee   You gotta get out of here. Both of yer.

Mark   Why's that?

Lee   Lawrie's on the warpath, I don't know if I can hold him back.

Mark   You've never tried.

Lee   Come on, not now.

Barry   He's gonna have a pop in front of everyone?

Lee   He doesn't care. Look, juss go, awright.

Barry   Mark?

Mark   We're stayin.

Lee   He's gonna do some damage.

Mark   It's nice to know you care.

Lee   Yer my best mate.

Mark   Were.

Lee   Are!

Mark   Then why'd you say it, Lee?

Lee   I'm sorry, fer fuck's sake.

Mark   If that walrus wants to have a pop, let 'im.

A brick comes smashing through one of the windows.

Phil   Oh fuck!

Jason   Jesus!

Gina   Dad!

Phil   I'm cut.

Jimmy (*sees the window*)   Christ.

Phil   Bastards!

Gina   You awright, Phil?

Phil   Do I look it?

Gina   Glen, get me the first-aid box.

Alan (*peers out of the window*)   You had better get the police as well. There is a whole army of black kids out there.

Jason (*looks out*)   Jesus!

Another brick comes flying through.

Oi! You black cunt.

Lee   Shut up, Jase.

Jason   They're lobbing bricks at us, wat you expect me to say?

Lee   I'm going out there.

Lawrie (*concerned*)   Lee?

Lee   You stay.

Alan   Lawrence. (*To* **Lee**.) He'll be all right.

Mark   Lee, hold up, mate.

Lee   Jimmy, call the police.

Gina   Tell them if they step one foot in my pub, they'll be murders.

Mark *and* **Lee** *go out.* **Gina** *treats* **Phil**'s *wounds with the first-aid box.*

Becks (*looks through the window*)   Thass the little sod who took Glen's phone.

Glen *runs behind the bar and goes upstairs.*

Gina   Glen, come back here, Glen!

Phil   He'll be awright. He's a good kid.

Gina   Oi, stop lookin at my tits.

Phil   I can't help it. They're lovely.

Gina   Excuse me?

Phil   Yer lovely.

Gina   Am I now?

Phil   Yeah.

Gina   You don't half pick yer moments, Philip.

Jimmy *approaches holding* **Glen** *by his ear.*

Jimmy   He was only trying to sneak out through the back door.

Gina   Wat you playing at?

Glen   It's my problem right, I'm gonna deal wid dem.

Jimmy   Listen to him.

Glen   Wat you moanin for?

Jimmy   There's a whole bleedin tribe out there, you wanna take them on? I've got a good mind to throw you out there myself.

Gina   You wanna do summin? Go change the loo rolls in the Gents.

Glen *goes to do as he is told.*

Gina   You call the police?

Jimmy   They're comin.

Becks   Might not need 'em now. Lee is doing the business, tellin them to back off.

Phil   Send one of dem bastards in here, I'll do the business on them.

Lawrie   Is Lee awright?

Becks   He's doing the business. (*To* **Barry**.) And yer Mark. They make a good team.

Gina (*shouts by door*)   Mark? Lee? You find the bastards who broke my winder and tell them they owe me money.

Some of the crowd shout obscenities at **Gina**.

Yeah, fuck you an 'all. (*Shuts the door.*)

Mark *and* **Lee** *come back in.*

Barry   You awright, bruv?

Mark   Yeah. Thanks ever so much for helpin out there, Gina, very useful.

Gina   I weren't jokin, Mark, I want money for my winders.

Mark   It coulda bin worse.

Lee   They were well pissed.

Mark   Speakin of which. (*Goes to the loo.*)

Lee   I don't know how long me and Mark held them off for, they could come back. You call the police?

Jimmy   On way.

Gina   You sure that will do any good?

Lee   I dunno.

He catches sight of **Lawrie** *who looks like he's heading for the Gents.*

Lawrie? Lawrie!

Lawrie *in fact detours slightly and goes to the cigarette machine. Where he buys a packet of fags.*

Lawrie (*as calm as you like*)   Wat? (*Walks back to the pool table.*)

On the screen, Keegan is being interviewed.

Jimmy   Wass he goin on about, Jase?

Jason   He's only fuckin quit.

Phil   Wat?

Jason   Straight up, Keegan's quit!

Phil   Muppet.

Jimmy   Jesus.

Becks   Gotta tell Rob. (*Dials.*) Rob! Yeah, I know, shit game. Listen, Keegan's quit. He bloody has, it's juss come on. Yer bloody booin musta got to him. (*Aside.*) They don't know.

Jason   Course they don't know, they won't know till they leave the stadium.

Becks (*to phone*)   Well, I won't miss him, dozy sod. Yeah we'll see yer in a bit. (*Hangs up.*) Wass Keegan sayin, wass he moanin about?

Alan   He's going on about how he can't do it no more.

Becks   Bloody girl.

Lawrie   Wat? He said wat?

Becks   Summin about him wantin to spend time wid his family.

Lawrie *throws his drink. It almost hits the screen.*

Gina   Lawrie! Thass our screen.

Jimmy   Yer lucky you didn't hit it. Oi, I'm talkin to you, Lawrie? If yer old man was still alive, he'd tan yer arse.

Lawrie   Keegan's got no backbone, Jimmy, this whole country's lost its spine.

Jimmy   Oh piss off

Lawrie   We ruled the world.

Lee (*approaching*)   Broth.

Lawrie   Go play wid yer monkey friends.

Becks   Ease up, Lawrie.

Lawrie   Did I ask yer for anything?

Becks (*scared*)   Nuh, mate, you didn't.

Lawrie *catches* **Barry***'s eye.*

Lawrie   You wanna have a pop? Well, come on then, black boy, show us how English you are.

Lee   Back off, Barry.

Barry   He challenged me.

Lee   He'll kill yer.

Lawrie   I'll have you, then those monkeys out there.

Gina *gets her baseball bat from behind the bar and waves it around.*

Becks   Whoa!

Gina   Not in my pub, you understand? Be told.

Jason   Yeah, Gina, watever you say.

Phil   I'm told.

Alan   Lawrie? (*Motions him to come over.*) Here!

Lee   Don't.

Gina   Leave him alone, Lee. He's a big boy.

Lawrie (*approaching*)   Why didn't you say anything?

Alan   Why won't you listen?

Lawrie   Cos I can't. Awright!

Alan   You won't even give yourself a chance. The smart-arses want to write you off as a brainless wanker, and you're letting them.

Lawrie   Juss let me have 'em. I won't mess up, I ain't stupid like that kid in Reading.

Alan   What do you know about Reading?

Lawrie   Got it from Lee. If this kid got himself caught, then thass his lookout.

Alan   The kid's name was Brian.

Lawrie   You gonna let me?

Alan   You remind me of him. Short fuse, kept running off on his own.

Lawrie   Come on, Alan.

Alan   He wouldn't listen. And I don't have time for people who refuse to listen, Lawrence!

Lawrie   Well, I'm tired of waiting. I wanted him. He wanted me. They all want it. Ask any coon. Let's juss stop all this fuckin about, and get it on. Lass one standing at the final whistle, wins England.

Alan   You gotta trust me, my way is the way forward.

Lawrie   No wonder this Brian kid got pissed off with yer. I mean fer fuck's sake, Alan, d'yer really think those smart-arses are gonna let us be as clever as them? I don't even want it.

Glen *is changing the loo paper in the Gents.* **Mark** *comes out of the next cubicle.*

Mark   You awright?

Glen *is getting frustrated as he cannot seem to get the finished loo roll off.*

Mark   Let me help.

Glen   No.

Mark   Don't be silly, there's nuttin to it.

Glen   Move.

Glen *shoves him, and as he does, a long kitchen knife drops from inside his jacket, on to the floor. He picks it quickly, but* **Mark** *has already seen it.*

Mark   Wat you doin wid that? Do you want me to go out and get yer mum, wat you doin wid that?

Glen   They fuck wid me, I'm gonna fuck wid them.

Mark   No, no that ain't the way, Glen.

Glen   You lot, you think yer so fuckin bad, I'll show you who's bad.

Mark   But this ain't the way. Duane and Tyrone yeah, they're juss boys. Not black boys, but juss boys. Stupid boys.

Glen   They're on us every day at school, all the white kids. Cos they think they're bad.

Mark   They're stupid boys, Glen.

Glen   You gonna move?

Mark   We are not all the same.

Glen   Move.

Mark   Juss gimme the knife.

Mark *moves to disarm him,* **Glen** *dodges* **Mark***, and stabs him repeatedly in the stomach.* **Mark** *drop to the floor.* **Glen** *cannot quite take in what he has done. He dashes out. Goes upstairs.*

Gina   You finished? Glen? Fine, ignore me why don't yer.

Lawrie *pops to the loo. He sees* **Mark***'s bleeding body and comes rushing out.*

Lawrie   We gotta go.

Alan   I don't waste time on losers, Lawrie, piss off.

Lawrie   Alan! We gotta go.

Alan   What have you done?

Lawrie   Nothing.

Jason *(comes running out of the loo)*   Oh shit!

Gina   Wat?

Jason   It's Mark.

Barry   Bruv? *(Sees* **Mark***.)* Mark!

Lee   Don't touch him.

Barry   Get off me.

Lee   Let me see, let me see.

Barry   Ambulance!

Lee   Barry, listen . . .

Barry   Get off me.

Gina   Christ!

Lee   Get out.

Barry   Help him.

Lee   Barry, he's dead, look at me, he's dead.

Barry   Who fuckin did it!

Lee *spots* **Phil** *and* **Becks** *trying to leave.*

Lee   Ware you going? You can't leave.

Phil   Oh, come on, mate.

Lee   No one leaves! Who was last in here?

Lawrie (*feels* **Alan**'s *stare*)   Wat?

Lee   Lawrie?

Lawrie   Oh yeah, here we go.

Lee   You were lass in the toilets.

Lawrie   It weren't me.

Alan   You bloody fool.

Lawrie   Alan, it weren't me, I saw him thass all.

Barry *runs at* **Lawrie**, *who holds him down, hitting him twice in the face.* **Lee** *pulls him off.*

Lee   Lawrie, enough, get off him.

Lawrie   I'm gonna line you up next to him.

Lee   Where's the knife, wat you do with it?

Lawrie *spits in his brother's face.*

Lee   Lawrence Bishop. I am arrresting you on suspicion of murder, you do not have to say anything, but it may harm yer defence if you do not mention when questioned something you may rely on in court. (**Lawrie** *spits in his face again.*) Anything you do say will be given in evidence. You made me choose.

Jason   This is fucked up.

Becks   Let us go, Lee.

Lee   No.

Jimmy *comes out, dragging* **Glen** *behind him.*

Gina   Dad?

Jimmy   Gina.

Gina   Wat? Wat!

Jimmy *throws the bloodstained knife on to the bar.*

Gina   No!

Becks   Oh shit.

Lee   Glen, come here.

Gina   No, Glen!

Lee   I said come here.

Barry   It was you!

Lee   Barry, juss back off, yeah.

Barry   Don't you fuckin touch me!

Glen   He's a black bastard, they all are.

Gina   Shut up.

Jimmy   Jesus.

Gina   Hard enuff for yu now, Dad?

Jimmy   Gina?

Alan   Rivers of blood.

Barry   Yu shut yer mout, I'll kill yer. I'll kill all of yer. Come on, come on! Who wants me, come on! Yer fuckin white cunts, all of yer! All of yer. Cunts! Come on! Yer white cunts.

Lee   Barry?

Barry   No.

He wipes the paint off his face.

No! No. (**Lee** *approaches.*) Fuck off. Get away from me.

Lawrie   Monkey lover.

Jason (*peers through window*)   Oh shit, they're only coming back.

Phil   Who?

Jason   Fuckin blacks.

Lawrie   No point playin games, Alan.

Alan   I don't know you.

Lawrie   No matter what, it'll come to this.

Sound of police sirens approaching.

Lee   Barry?

Barry   No.

Lee (*to* **Barry**)   Don't lose yerself.